Praise for *Deliver What You Promise*

'Every day I think about how Bali would do things. My company is 100% run in the Bali Padda style.'

Niels Duedahl, CEO, Norlys

'Bali Padda's mind and writing shed light on some of the most complex challenges faced by organisations. There are two kinds of leaders: those who ask for clarity, and those who bring clarity — the consumers of control, and the producers of purpose. In today's uncertain, volatile and complex world we need more of the latter. Bali Padda stands out in this rare category.'

Yves Morieux, Managing Director and Senior Partner, Boston Consulting Group (BCG), director of the BCG Institute for Organization

'An amazing book about how mastering the supply chain became a fundamental pillar to save LEGO and to make it a formidable company. Also, a personal story about a operations executive becoming an extremely powerful contributor to the success of the C-level team that led LEGO from near bankruptcy to global success. It is probably the most needed book today for companies facing unprecedented supply chain disruptions.'

Carlos Cordon, IMD Professor of Strategy and Supply Chain Management

DELIVER WHAT YOU PROMISE

As Chief Operations Officer at LEGO from 2005, and in earlier operational roles from 2003, Bali Padda played a decisive role in the recovery and growth of this iconic toy firm. Bali and his colleagues executed a remarkable turnaround, from a near-terminal crisis to a return to profit within 18 months. In 2016, Bali was asked to step in as CEO of the LEGO Group while a search for a new CEO was initiated, becoming the company's first non-Danish CEO.

Currently, Bali Padda is a highly sought-after business adviser and mentor to C-suite executives.

DELIVER WHAT YOU PROMISE

BALI PADDA

Heligo
Books

First published in the UK by Heligo Books
An imprint of Bonnier Books UK
4th Floor, Victoria House,
Bloomsbury Square,
London, WC1B 4DA

Owned by Bonnier Books
Sveavägen 56, Stockholm, Sweden

twitter.com/heligobooks

Trade Paperback – 978-1-788706-72-8
Ebook – 978-1-788706-73-5
Audio – 978-1-788706-71-1

A CIP catalogue of this book is available from the British Library.

Designed by www.envydesign.co.uk
Printed and bound in Australia by Griffin Press

1 3 5 7 9 10 8 6 4 2

Heligo Books is an imprint of Bonnier Books UK
www.bonnierbooks.co.uk

Sati, Ajay and Avneet – this is for you.
Thanks for tolerating an absent husband and father.
I could not have embarked on this journey without your
support, understanding and encouragement.
Heartfelt thanks.

Contents

Preface

It is early autumn 2005. LEGO is on the brink. One more bad Christmas and the toy firm beloved by millions around the world could be history. The Kristiansen family, who have owned the company since 1932, have financed the payroll for the past 12 months after historic losses in 2004. The burning platform is the metaphor of choice among colleagues fighting for the firm's survival and the flames are just a few feet away. Demand for toys is higher than the year before across most ranges of products, which is a relief and an opportunity, but also a challenge: the firm has to up its game to meet expectations. Failure to deliver would be devastating, almost certainly fatal to the firm's very existence and the salaries of everyone in the room.

The following exchange takes place in a weekly gathering dubbed the Visual Factory, that was instituted at the firm by the author, as a senior supply chain executive in 2003. It involves all the key disciplines – supply chain, manufacturing, sales, marketing, finance – standing in a room (no chairs at all) for just half an hour or so, early morning once a week, a gathering so punctual and focused we close the doors to late entrants. We physically write the crucial data on the walls, limiting ourselves to just that information that is necessary to deliver – what we call the 'Vital Few'. The entire value chain is represented; the idea is that an experienced individual can understand the state of operations by reading the information on the walls. Gathered in one place are the data and the key people responsible for raw material supply, for moulding machines, manufacture and distribution; for design, marketing, selling, finance and customer service. There is no hierarchy and departmental rivalry is discouraged; there may be someone newly qualified from college in their first role, stood next to the CEO. At each gathering, the individual responsible has to say whether or not the targets have been reached, the promises have been met. The meeting is run by exception: if on target, there is no dialogue. There's no hiding behind screens. There are no screens.

This particular morning, there is evidence of progress; equally, there is evidence of uncertainty. There is a need to manage the mood, as well as the supply-and-demand mechanics. You cannot take the emotion out of the room where everyone's livelihood is at stake. You have to harness it, allied to reason; to stay calm, be factual, address the real issues.

Preface

Five minutes before the discussion opens – 7:25am. There is frantic activity – several people with red and green board markers in hand are updating the latest metrics on the whiteboards. Others are reviewing the boards as they enter the room.

Everyone is standing. By 7:30 there are around 20 people in the room, from all disciplines. The chairman looks at the clock on the wall and shuts the door. All four walls of the room are covered with whiteboards.

There is a flow to the discussion, starting with the customer: what do they need, by when?

A new manager, recruited from a fast-moving global consumer goods company and attending her first Visual Factory, stays silent. She watches closely, listens, round-eyed with fascination.

In the Visual Factory, the data are updated where necessary each week. The metrics chosen are determined twice a year based on the things that really matter to the customers' business and to the supplier. Metrics are handwritten – no printouts are allowed. There are no minutes from previous meetings. Actions taken are handwritten on one of the whiteboards. The meeting starts with due actions from the previous meeting. If completed, they are erased; if not, a red asterisk is placed against the due date – to be followed up the next week.

There are no formal routine updates from different departments; discussion is limited to prioritised tasks. At this particular meeting there is an action for sales to follow through with a retail customer on a Black Friday programme. In order to meet the projected volumes, the supply side has requested a commitment from the customer prior to the meeting. The head of supply chain speaks: 'Has the customer committed yet?'

'We're waiting for confirmation, should be any day. Technically, we've just passed the "last-last" timing, but . . .'

'Has he committed?'

'Well, it's not really a "yes or no" situation at the moment . . .'

'Actually, it is. The last-last date has passed.'

'In that case, it's a no at the moment but . . .'

'OK, then LEGO does not participate in the Black Friday programme.'

There is silence in the room. Several people appear to be on the brink of commenting. No one wants to be first. Eventually, someone says: 'We *cancel*?'

'Yes,' the head of supply chain is certain, solid in tone.

There is another silence, more intense than the last. Still, the new manager remains quiet, though the look of intrigued fascination seems to intensify on her face.

It is a big decision. This is one of the top three retail customers, with branches in every city and many towns across North America. There will be consequences, *big* consequences. Customer service is always the first priority at the Visual Factory: delivering what you promise. The red-coded fill rates to the customer orders are a priority but it works both ways: the customer has to provide confirmation of the order with sufficient notice. This prompts a further animated discussion. Someone from sales says: 'We need to be more agile. Supply needs to be able to scale up and down more.'

'We've been doing that the past couple of years,' the head of supply chain replies. 'It's why we're losing money. The forecasts are too inaccurate. When we're not able to deliver, we need to understand why in more detail.'

'The first priority is to be flexible.'

'No, the first priority is to be reliable. Deliver what we promise. Reliability first, flexibility second. If we need to order extra moulds we need to know and we need to maintain quality. Flexibility is a by-product of better matching between demand and supply.'

A further discussion on reasoning for misses is played out and takes place between a vice-president and a supply planner. In the quick exchange it is determined that there is a shortage of parts in manufacturing that hampered the order being filled to the required standard. The recovery date is agreed and action captured. Another customer discussion plays out around forecasting and demand planning, where it emerges that the demand was three times the forecast. It will take more than four weeks to recover on this and the sales team is requested to relay this to the customer. Action is captured on the whiteboard.

There is a clear feeling of discomfort in the room – having to give bad news to the customer. But this is the reality: it has to be done and will be followed up the next week.

The new manager is wondering whether to speak. She has never seen a head of supply chain have such an influence over a retail manufacturing operation. This is a very different way of holding discussions, a different way of leading and a very different way of operating – the focus and transparency are startling . . .

Chapter 1

Understand Your Customer's Motives

The squeal of delight when a child opens their desired LEGO toy on Christmas Day requires a network of specialists, coordinated with orchestral precision, to deliver. They have spent their careers dedicated to learning their specialised tasks: from sourcing the polymer feed material to manufacturing the moulds for the parts, crafting precise instructions, ensuring quality and correct packing, supplying the retailers. They have displayed exceptional care and diligence to ensure that the pieces in that Christmas Day giftbox fit as expected, with no missing pieces or wrong colours.

This book describes the disciplines required for such execution: the collaboration, accountability, transparency and executive discipline, while understanding the business as a complex organism. These were lessons I learned early in my managerial career. I had the opportunity to implement them as part of a team of executives who rescued the LEGO company from near-bankruptcy in the early 2000s – a period that featured missing parts and problems in delivery. We oversaw a return to growth, resulting in the firm becoming the most-loved – and most profitable – toy company in the world. In some surveys, it has emerged as the most-loved brand across the whole economy.

We often read that we are living through a period of increasing change in the world of business. The rapid rise of artificial intelligence and digital, platform-based business models in the first few decades of the twenty-first century has created such turmoil that businesses have to become agile, and data-driven, in order to survive and grow. It is the Fourth Industrial Revolution. This widely accepted perspective is simultaneously valid, yet potentially deceptive. It is valid because technological and market changes are indeed creating relentless turbulence, but possibly deceptive in the way in which it is understood. Firstly, it never was the case that economic life was orderly and predictable. I have been in business management for 40 years and the first two decades of my career were characterised by momentous political, technological and economic change, featuring highly unpredictable dynamics. Secondly, while businesses do have to be agile, their first priority is delivery. As I write, it is likely that there are plenty of hi-tech, digital, agile businesses that are going bust and it is probable that, in many or most of these cases, they will go belly-up because they fail to honour the timeless principles about how to run a business.

The approach described in this book is centred around the principles of disciplined execution, an illustration of which features in the Preface before the astonished gaze of the new executive from the fast-moving consumer goods sector: focus, transparency, accountability, collaboration; minimising the impact of waste, waffle and ego. Yet there were even earlier lessons that I learned in my somewhat unconventional career and they involved the importance of fairness and assertiveness and the art of negotiating.

In common with many immigrants, my first working experience was in the family store, as a teenager. Kent is popularly known as the Garden of England, but Gravesend in the 1960s and 1970s was not, it's fair to say, the prettiest corner of the garden. It lies 20 miles to the east of London, near the mouth of the river Thames. The riverside train station had been closed, and the building was boarded up, along with other riverside buildings. In the years since, the riverside area has been smartly gentrified, with numerous bars and restaurants having been opened, but back then some sections were rather drab. The neighbouring town of Northfleet featured wharves, cement works, quarries and a cable factory. It was as industrial as any part of England. The mile-wide estuary was one of the busiest shipping lanes in the world, with merchant ships, and the occasional passenger liner, passing in and out of the Ports of London and Tilbury.

Our family had a shop in the High Street near the river and I would sometimes encounter a sailor who had come across on the river ferry to Gravesend from Tilbury and they would ask the way. Directions were always done by naming the pub – there was a pub on almost every corner: 'Right at the Foresters Arms, left at the Prince Albert,' and so on.

We had moved to England from Mumbai (formerly Bombay), Maharashtra state, a tropical cosmopolitan city in south-western India, when I was 12. I often felt homesick. My pastimes in India involved flying kites and, inevitably, street cricket, and during April and May eating fresh mangoes. I missed the mango season and the start of monsoons the most. Hardest of all in England was the harsh reality of racism. But you did not experience this from everyone, it was very unpredictable. The reaction of local people to Asian immigrants ran the full range from kindness and hospitality to the most appalling abuse. On one occasion, I stood at a street corner in the centre of town and a cyclist spat at me. I felt anger and tears well up inside me. As a 12-year-old, I could not understand why this was done. It was in contrast with the accepting atmosphere in the diverse suburb of Mumbai in which I had lived; I had assumed that England would be similarly accepting, I soon learnt that it was not!

Understand Your Customer's Motives

We lived above the family shop, which was a speciality Indian grocery store, mostly serving the local Asian community, on the High Street, which in Gravesend is a quite narrow street of mostly small shops and cafes that runs slightly downhill towards the river, at right angles to the wider New Street, which hosts the department stores and other larger shops. It was expected that from a young age I should help in the shop in my spare time. I did not mind – and as it turned out, this provided an excellent grounding in some key business disciplines. I learned so much: how to manage stock, the importance of cash flow. I also learned to combine a service ethic with assertiveness. The mantra that 'the customer is always king' requires interpretation, I learned. The customer is transactional; your interests overlap, but they are not the same. You provide a good service; you delight the customer, but you maintain margins sufficient for a good living and protect your own interests. You do not necessarily cede to every demand a consumer makes, yet if a loyal customer suggests a discount for a large purchase, you seek ways to accommodate them. It is a relationship based on negotiation and mutual respect, not excessive subservience: the customer is king, but not an autocrat.

Years later, understanding this principle helped me in LEGO. In manufacturing operations, the direct customer you are dealing with is the retailer. A retailer may wish to order more of your most popular products than they can realistically sell and at a low price. This has implications for the supplier. Everything is a negotiation.

Yet assertiveness must never become aggression or exploitation. Again, this principle was ingrained in childhood, from family values, and from the morality fables of Indian cinema. My family were exceptionally entrepreneurial and in addition to running the shop, we would hire the local ABC cinema and one in Erith in south-east London and screen Bollywood movies, selling tickets to the local Asian community. Nowadays from the UK you can access dozens of Indian channels via satellite television, but none of that was around in the 1970s. A theme in many of these films was karma: in particular, how if you cheat people, it comes back to bite you. I watched more of these movies than most and we applied this principle when running the store: always to be fair; for example, to pay suppliers punctually and be honest in your dealings.

Those two early lessons, about being fair and being assertive in equal measure are, of course, common sense. But I discovered much later in my career that it can be difficult for experienced managers to maintain these disciplines when under pressure, when tempted by an opportunity to boost profile or ego, when caught up in emotionally charged politics or complex interpersonal dynamics. They are priceless principles; they will never go out of fashion and they require constant discipline.

Applying the lessons at LEGO

When I took over a senior supply chain managerial role at LEGO North America in the early 2000s, much of this grounding remained highly relevant. I encountered a supply chain, and indeed a whole business, in some disarray. Some of the strategic missteps and their correction will be discussed in later chapters. Of pressing concern to us in operations was a mismatch between supply and demand. At one point we were moving more stock between our distribution centres than from the centres to the stores. We had insufficient supply of popular, or potentially popular, toys and over-supply of unpopular sets. It was like a grocery store with bags of rice going past their sell-by date, packages of food no one wanted, and no lentils. I could perceive several weaknesses that were inter-related:

- Insufficient research on consumer preferences.
- Influence of apparently untested assumptions, for example: 'The toy industry doesn't make money between January and July' and 'Urban and family-themed sets won't sell in North America'.
- Pressure from retailers to over-supply in the run-up to Christmas, resulting in heavy discounting in January, waste and damaging of the brand.
- Weak negotiating skills exacerbating the excessively pro-cyclical pattern.

These weaknesses were inter-related; lack of detailed knowledge of demand and preferences in the consumer market impaired our ability to negotiate effectively with retailers. There were untested hypotheses about the market. The narrative that: 'The toy industry doesn't make money from January to July' seemed potentially to be a self-fulfilling prophesy. While there would always be seasonality, because of the importance of the Christmas gift-buying period for the toy industry, this mantra was accepted all too easily. Analysis of the data confirmed this. Some of us could see a clear pattern in which stores were over-supplied in the run-up to Christmas, and then products had to be heavily discounted by retailers in the New Year, in order to clear their stock. This resulted in multiple problems for the producer: thin margins in the early part of the year, the costs of excessive production, accentuated seasonality not justified by actual demand, potential for waste with environmental implications and damaged reputation of the brand through discounting.

Our sales and marketing people were saying, 'Make what we forecast.' Retail customers would pressure us to meet optimistic projections of Christmas demand. Negotiating skills within operations needed strengthening, both internally when dealing with sales and marketing, and externally with the retailers. The motive of the head of purchasing for a major department store was not to guarantee good margins for the toy firm, it was to gain market share of LEGO toys compared with a competitor. This is an important distinction and an illustration of how our interests overlapped but were not the same. I seemed to grasp this more clearly than others. We had good retail sales data so if we were selling ten units over a period, some of us began arguing we should supply around ten, rather than double that, which had been the practice. Ultimately, this would be in the interests of the retailers also.

At a key period in the turnaround, in late 2005 at the time of my promotion to a global role as chief operations officer (COO), I penned a 'Letter to the New Organisation'. Here, I argued that we should work back from what the customer wants and tailor our operations and supply towards that. It sounds logical and straightforward, but as a discipline it can be difficult to stick to. I had tough negotiations externally with our retail customers and internally with our own sales and marketing executives.

It was considered eccentric for a supply chain executive to meet customers and attend trade fairs, but I insisted on doing so. As I will discuss in later chapters, everything is interconnected and every function has a role. I would meet directly with retail customers, not leaving this to the sales function alone, and I attended the industry toy fairs. Over time, I developed good relationships with senior buyers at Walmart, Target and Toys R Us. Years later, our head of

IT said to me: 'I've never before seen a supply chain guy more passionate about the consumers than the sales guys.'

Meeting fans of LEGO

Challenging the untested assumptions about consumer preferences was a shared enterprise, over several years, with other executives. After I was appointed to a global role as chief operating officer in 2005, I formed a close partnership with Mads Nipper, head of marketing. Those of us in the leadership team also met LEGO fans, a most fascinating experience. There would be conventions, organised by the fans themselves, not the company. Jørgen Vig Knudstorp, chief executive between 2004 and 2016, other members of the senior team including Mads, the owner Kjeld Kirk Kristiansen and myself, visited several, from 2004 onwards, and many fans were naturally delighted to meet senior executives from the company. There is an established fanbase called Adult Fans of LEGO, whose members will pay a healthy fee to attend a convention of three or four days. They know more about the product than I did myself. Talking with them provided insights into the importance of the brick and the versatility of the best-designed models and sets. At one such meeting, I was asked what my favourite LEGO toy had been when I was growing up. I replied that my childhood had not involved much play, apart from music, that I had had to help in the family store and never owned a LEGO set. Their reply was that I must have had a deprived childhood, not to have played with LEGO! That was just one illustration of their passion. To have such dedicated fans, who are not mere consumers but advocates for the brand, is a priceless asset and it was a highly useful exercise to meet them.

Listening to head of marketing Mads Nipper talk to the fans was fascinating and instructive; his lens was different to mine and in some ways closer to that of the fans. He would pick up something that helped him into the next design phase and I was picking up what helps from operations.

In another initiative, market researchers from LEGO arranged to lodge with families – typically for a few days, informing reports that guided product development and design. This kind of research yields insights that are difficult to glean from questionnaire replies, because the researcher can make observations on behaviour. One example of such an insight is that a child likes to have 'little victories' – for example, completing a small car as part of a large and complex LEGO set. This resulted in our creation of numbered bags for components, relating to the order of putting the pieces together.

As Mads says, in an interview for this book: 'That's what I call the finer details of the play experience, which I think is super important for the totality of the experience.'

During the turnaround period, we identified that there was untapped demand for some long-established product lines, such as DUPLO and LEGO City. There is increasing awareness in business that 'retro' products can retain their appeal, or experience a revival. New isn't always better. The particular case of LEGO City illustrated this vividly; it offers a classic case of an untested hypothesis harming development of a traditional product. It was one of the long-standing brands that was comparatively neglected in terms of marketing spend in a period of diversification of LEGO products in the mid-1990s to early 2000s.

LEGO City, as the name suggests, is the brand for a range of models that feature urban settings, ranging from a fire station to ski villages. It began in the 1970s under the LEGO Town brand, at the time that the first minifigures were introduced. The predominant view when I joined LEGO was that LEGO City would have limited appeal in the US, where there would be a cultural preference for action and hero figures. Yet this assumption about the US market had never really been tested. It probably came from a cultural stereotype about America resting on the global awareness of Hollywood action movies, Westerns and car chases. Yet when Mads decided to challenge this assumption, and we began to market LEGO City more to US consumers, we found that demand took off. Of course, within the LEGO City stable there has always been reinvention and innovation, as the brand covers many different models.

Most intriguingly, detailed research from around the world into consumer preferences found remarkably little regional variation. There is a marked difference here compared with sectors such as clothing and home décor, where national and regional preferences differ considerably and marketing and manufacturing have to reflect this. Our researchers found that in some countries there is considerable apartment living, high work ethic and less time and space for creative play. We expected that this would result in differing preferences for the size and type of LEGO models preferred, but in practice, it did not. For the LEGO fan, the family's preferences in Shanghai will be similar to those in Dallas, Lagos, Munich and Mumbai. The impulse to *play* is, according to neuroscientists, one of the seven core human emotions: it is a universal desire.

Mads recalls the misconception that he challenged that US boys only liked action figures and that therefore LEGO City would have limited appeal in the US. He adds: 'I simply refused to believe that, because what we found out was that, in reality, in many cases children's play behaviour was a lot more alike across the world than what their parents believed. A lot more . . . I refused to believe that we can't have a global assortment, because no insights that we gained revealed any evidence at all that there were differences to the play behaviour of children and we said then that if children like that then it's a matter of time before their parents become convinced.

'They [LEGO designers] said "OK, we will get the City products [for the US market], but we need a New York Fire Department truck, we need a different fire truck than the one that looks like a German one and they obviously look very different." And then, back to the same insight: I don't buy that. I simply don't believe it, because children, when you showed them the German fire truck, they absolutely loved it.'

Through our interaction with LEGO fans, we continually improved the service at our call centres. They are staffed by employees who are similarly knowledgeable and passionate about LEGO as the fans themselves and who go through extensive training so that they can help the callers on their varied requests. Access to such personal, human help is an essential part of the service. Call centres for the consumer – at least on products as personal and creative as LEGO models – should never be automated.

The way in which a company handles a complaint says much about its culture and values. It is human nature to view a complaint as a nuisance and an imaginative alternative to view it as an opportunity to learn and to improve service and quality. There is even some research indicating that an angry customer can become highly engaged and loyal, if their complaint is handled well.[1] The key aspect to bear in mind is this: the way in which you handle a complaint will be the subject of vibrant discussion, at the customer's home and by the water cooler in their workplace, whether you handle it well or badly. It is, counter-intuitively, a chance to shine.

In the recovery phase at LEGO, we deepened our knowledge of demand and preferences in the consumer markets to help us better match supply to demand. We began asking ourselves tough questions; challenging untested assumptions, engaging in more in-depth research into actual consumer preferences.

We also learned to negotiate effectively with retailers. We learned not to go into discount stores and we curbed the extent of discounting in the January sales. Understanding the retail customer as a merchant was central to the negotiations. CEO Jørgen Vig Knudstorp placed emphasis on understanding the 'money-making logic'. We had ours; Walmart, Target and Amazon had theirs. They were in competition with each other, so each retailer wanted to have the biggest market share within retail of LEGO toys. Distribution was significantly simplified and improved by consolidating into just three centres – Europe, North America and Asia. Around 2017, one retail customer said to me, 'Bali, I have envied you how you have managed this. The one year you listened to me I lost money. That story is in the business.'

Summary

There is a certain circularity in my career: I give advice to CEOs as a consultant that is informed not only by my own experience as a senior executive, but also by my earliest dealings nearly half a century earlier as a boy in a family-owned grocery store. The differences between being chief executive of a successful global company and helping in the shop on a Saturday are obvious, the similarities much less so. I have always sought to be diligent and ambitious when in low-income roles and diligent and humble as a senior executive. Ultimately, a business exists to serve a human need, so its orientation, and the application of everyone in the enterprise, must be geared to that. This means that the principles of understanding the customer, meeting their needs, of fairness and assertiveness in negotiations are timeless and will always be central.

Key principles from this chapter

- Customers are sovereign, but don't let them become the autocrat.
- Delivery is ultimately more important than flexibility; a well-informed, well-managed enterprise will naturally be agile as it responds to changes in demand and technology.

- Customers in business-to-business relationships have their money-making logic, you have yours. Understanding this is key to understanding behaviour and as a guide in negotiations.

How to implement the principles

- Work back from the customer's needs to determine priorities.
- Always test your hypotheses, be particularly careful to avoid cultural stereotypes.
- Discover what the consumers, and potential consumers, actually want. If there is a widely accepted premise or belief, check to see if it is rooted in evidence.
- Remember that customers are agents with different priorities to yourselves as providers. Your interests overlap but they are not the same.

Chapter 2
Innovation is a Way of Thinking

Management is a science, a craft and an art. It is essential to be guided by robust and relevant data and evidence where you can (the science), but this is not always possible and you sometimes need to deploy the practical wisdom of practitioners (the craft), while being open to the potential or necessity to completely reinvent your business model and ways of working (the art). These skills are both essential and complementary; emphasising which to deploy and in which mix depends upon context. Businesses get into enormous difficulty if they neglect one or more of these three essential components – or if the emphasis is not well-suited for the context.

From a young age, I have studied work processes and practices and I have imagined different, better ways of doing things. It may be as much instinct as learning, given that I come from a highly entrepreneurial family. I would think about ways in which processes could be improved. I understood management as being a blend of innovation, execution and delivery forming a connected whole, rather than a choice between steady state and disruption. This began even before I became a manager, while still working as an operator. As a junior operator, working on production lines in the 1980s in Northfleet, England, I succeeded in annoying both managers and the trade unions when making my observations about how processes could be made smarter.

When we think of innovation in business, our minds are drawn to breakthrough inventions and disruptive technologies. A tangible invention tends to register more in the public consciousness than gradual progress. There are more statues and plaques commemorating individuals who have made contributions through patient work to improve services. An inventor such as Alan Turing or Elon Musk will have name recognition, whereas individuals who have transformed supply chain effectiveness or customer service will not attract a cult following. If you watch old and new Formula 1 videos on YouTube, you can see the evolution of Grand Prix pit stops from the 1950s to today. In the old days, pit stops would take up to a minute. The driver would have a drink, someone would even polish his windscreen. Today, that pit stop is three seconds. *Three seconds!* The same kind of evolution has taken place with production lines around the world. This kind of progress came about through the relentless reimagining and reworking of established processes to quicken each element, along the way harnessing technological developments, such as faster and more powerful tools for replacing a wheel, while improving and quickening teamwork. It follows from this that innovation is always an asset and in all disciplines, including supply, distribution and retail, not only in design, technology and marketing. That is, provided the innovation is geared to a rational purpose, to create something valuable and new, or better to deliver your promise to the customer.

In a healthy organisational culture, innovation can come from anywhere: production engineers devising ingenious new processes, customer-facing staff with ideas for smarter communication and more tailored service, and so on. A common notion that creativity and innovation belong solely within the more obviously creative-sounding disciplines such as design and technological research is unhelpful. It is linked to a misleading concept of certain business functions – design, marketing, strategy – being defined as 'value-adding', compared with 'utility' or 'cost-based' functions such as supply and logistics, a prejudice that will be challenged in later chapters. When we talk about an innovative culture within a business, this applies to *everyone*, not just the research and development functions.

Innovation does not necessarily imply disruption, but also a constant quest for improvement. The innovator's mind is restless; not assuming that the way things are done is settled and must go unchallenged. It involves being relentlessly curious, adaptive and enquiring. This is always change for a purpose; evolution to meet a need, not gratuitous change or an initiative just for the sake of appearing to do something. There is an unfortunate tendency in management discussions to pose innovation and execution as opposing disciplines. Really, they are complementary. Discussion around disruptive technology supposes an inbuilt tension between a desire for 'steady state' against a perceived need for total reinvention of ways of doing things. This exaggerates the case at both ends of an imagined spectrum. Steady state never exists and reinvention often involves nurturing and preserving some elements while improving or radically changing others. In the digital age there is often a temptation to try to automate everything, a tendency I will challenge in Chapter 10 (*see also* pages 173–181). The real test with any innovation is: does the planned change enhance quality of life and create new opportunities for your ultimate customers? Is it practical? Working back from the customer's needs is the surest way to stay honest, relevant and business-like with innovation and adaptation. This can, of course, include internal customers.

Agility is not enough

A highly fashionable concept in business management in the 2020s, agility is also frequently misunderstood. In much current discussion on management, it seems to be discussed as a discrete target to aim for; that is, as an end in itself. We hear that: 'The business must be agile for the twenty-first century'. This is true up to a point, but agility does not stand alone as a quality – it is closely linked to other necessary disciplines. My experience indicates that agility is best understood as a by-product of smart strategy closely linked to effective operational ability. This approach explains the disciplines described in this book. If the business's leaders see the organisation as a complex organism; if strategy is approached as a process of discovery and iteration; if managers and their teams work back from the customer's needs; if there are functional leaders who can negotiate, assert and also collaborate; if they keep things simple and transparent with the Vital Few points of data – then the business will be agile. More importantly, it will be optimally agile, responding to real demand and emerging opportunities and technologies, not changing for change's sake.

By the same token, here are some still relatively common beliefs or practices that hinder true agility: seeing supply chain or manufacturing as 'dirty' or merely a cost base rather than a partner, managing by targets with little understanding of operations, long lists of financial incentives tied to Key Performance Indicators (KPIs), failure to involve all staff, quality assigned as the responsibility of a separate department, bureaucracy, excessive rivalry between departments that have to cooperate, too much data and long presentations at meetings.

'Deliver what you promise' is a timeless guide for operations and indeed everyone in management. A major hazard with highly innovative practices is to be over-ambitious and promise more than you can deliver. The discipline of innovators and strategists is to know what to promise and of operations to ensure delivery on the promise. Sustained failure in either discipline tends to be fatal for the company. Failure to innovate and adapt has led to some high-profile business collapses. Some retail stores, such as Woolworths, failed to adapt sufficiently to changing technologies and markets as online shopping grew and tastes changed. The video rental company Blockbuster was eclipsed by the online company Netflix which, with tragic irony, had offered to work in partnership with Blockbuster while it was still smaller and the larger company turned it down. The lesson here is that maintaining high levels of operational excellence with a business and technological model that is becoming outdated is obviously disastrous and such failures have attracted considerable media attention and much discussion in business schools. An appropriate level of agility and responsiveness is essential. This comes naturally to those who see strategy as evolution, not a rigid plan (*see also* Chapter 5, pages 91–5).

Innovation is a Way of Thinking

Arguably less obvious than the failure to adapt, but equally fatal for a business, is to have an innovative strategy and technology, but fail to set up operations effectively. For example, peer-to-peer lending is an innovation in finance that has seen considerable growth, but some start-ups have failed owing to misjudgements on risk, weak financial controls and other factors.[2] This is why, in the scene featured in the Preface to this book (page 5), the head of supply chain says: 'Reliability first, flexibility second,' in line with a finding from research by the Economist Intelligence Unit (*see also* discussion in Chapter 3, pages 52–3), which concluded that execution marks successful business leaders out more than strategy formulation 'because fewer corporate leaders are as skilled at it'.

Agility can sound like a benign and democratic feature. Sometimes, however, it has to be imposed. Prior to the turnaround at LEGO there could be observed the phenomenon known by the catchy saying 'paralysis by analysis' – too much open-ended discussion on processes and potential redesigns, and too much consequent delay, when the situation was urgent. As discussed later in Chapter 9 (*see also* pages 165–6), the platform was burning, but not everyone fully appreciated this. There is a tendency in Danish culture to prize consensus, but in emergencies there can be a need to be more directive. The purpose in this context was to become more responsive to the emerging reality;

in other words, become more agile – and to do so while strengthening the organisation's operational muscle.

A popular misconception is that maximising automation will cause a business to become more efficient and agile. This is a simplification of what should always be a sophisticated judgement, tailored for the context, and is the subject of Chapter 10 (*see also* pages 173–181).

The immigrant's eye

My earliest working experiences were typical of many immigrants: they involved a combination of working in the family store and taking relatively low-paid jobs in a factory. As a young adult, I embarked on a couple of entrepreneurial initiatives in retail, which did not succeed commercially, although they afforded some learning opportunities, as I shall discuss in Chapter 4 (see also pages 79–81). As a young married father, I had to be responsible and secure a regular wage but that did not mean that I switched off the innovator's eye. I took on a production line job at AEI Cables in Northfleet, Kent. Later, I began a similar production line job at the pharmaceutical company Wellcome in nearby Dartford. The pay was modest and much of the work was routine, but it was here that some opportunities opened up. Much of my early enquiry stemmed from being puzzled by practices I observed in the workplace that seemed illogical – or at least sub-optimal. They didn't seem to have passed a pragmatic test. I would ask questions – sometimes to others (which could get me into trouble), and sometimes just to myself, such as:

- Why are the people who are going to be working directly in a system not involved in its design?
- Why do we stick to the same approach for years, instead of continually seeking to improve it, like Formula 1 engineers at the pit stop?
- Why do we have forced separation of individuals when they need to form a team, yet forced togetherness in an aimless meeting when they do not?
- Why do many managers persist with a style of meeting that they do not like or find rewarding, that often performs neither a commercial nor a social purpose, or is at best inefficient?
- Why do many managers, including senior managers at a major corporation, sometimes make major changes based on hunches and untested hypotheses?
- How do narratives take possession of a managerial population based on superstitious notions such as 'not invented here' or 'flavour of the month'?
- Why, given that there was much evidence-based learning on offer from management thinkers such as Charles Handy, Peter Drucker and Tom Peters, was there such a gulf between the learning and practice? In short,

why was so much business management not evidence-based?

- Why are some managers content to be a victim, limiting themselves with narratives that diminish their own agency – their ability to change things?

Radical productivity improvement at Wellcome

My first promotion at Wellcome was to a managerial position, with around 60 people reporting to me. This was a major event in my early career. I recall thinking that, if there were no more promotions afterwards, this would be sufficient. However, I had no intention of simply coasting, basking in the joy of promotion. I wanted to make a difference: here was an opportunity to put into practice some of the ideas that I had been developing, both through my own observations and my studies. There was ample scope to improve teamwork, productivity and performance.

Being partially responsible for supply was a challenge at Wellcome because demand fluctuated considerably and quality requirements were the highest. We would receive tenders from the Middle East with strict deadlines and there would be a sudden rush – hence the need for overtime. Standards in pharma are among the strictest in the manufacturing world, for obvious reasons. You are subject to strict external inspections, of both policy and procedure. One lapse and you could lose your certification. Temperature has to be very strictly controlled. Security was a huge concern. Some types of prescription pills are taken recreationally and have been associated with addiction issues. Packaged tablets are comparatively small and easily smuggled, often with a high street-value. The security overseeing their manufacture and distribution was scarcely less than that required for cash or gold bullion. You weighed the consignment. It had to tally with the calibrated number of packages – the smallest inconsistency was not acceptable.

I could see potential improvements for speed and efficiency in production lines, but this obviously had to be without compromising quality. I had begun to learn, however, that with some of the smartest approaches to teamworking, harnessing everyone's contribution in a focused way, you could improve speed and quality simultaneously. This meant some internal battles, though: I would challenge issues if I felt they lacked logic.

My observation was that quality was the responsibility of everyone and this had been the concept of the early 'quality' pioneers such as the engineer and management consultant W. Edwards Deming in the 1950s. Deming's ideas were highly progressive and encouraged continual improvement throughout the enterprise. He opposed management by fear, management by financial targets and encouraged the widest possible collaboration, bound by a joint quest for continually improving quality. The

W. Edwards Deming Institute expresses this distinction well: 'Many of the [Deming] principles are philosophical. Others are more programmatic. All are transformative in nature.'[3] As I began my career in the 1980s, however, I found that the ideas had become corrupted by excessive hierarchy and a bureaucratic approach. Quality was often the responsibility of a separate 'Quality Department', which produced copious amounts of form-filling to support its activities. By separating the activity into a dedicated department and creating unnecessary bureaucracy, the concept can fail to live up to its promise. Through this succession of well-meaning but misguided small steps, a good idea can become a management fad and ultimately, in some cases, rejected, along with the good ideas that originally inspired the initiative.

I insisted on operators being included and helping to take responsibility for designing systems and processes. This was met with resistance. For example, on the production line I wanted to engage the fitter. The line engineer's (fitter's) role was to manage the mechanical running of the line and conduct changeovers to different formats. His supervisor did not want that so I invited him too. When there was a machine that needed servicing, it was the responsibility of the fitter whose 'turn' it was, but I wanted it to be the fitter who knew the machinery best. This proposal was met with opposition from the unions. It became political, and

I wasn't invited to certain meetings, but I eventually won that battle.

I wanted the individuals who were working the production line continuously to co-design the practices, in the way that Formula 1 engineers continually improve the speed, accuracy and efficiency of a tyre change. I took the view that operators were not stupid. As Tom Peters says, 'They do not hang their brains on the entrance to the workplace.' They were people who ran sports teams or pub quizzes in their spare time. Where was the logic in not asking them to contribute their ideas? It didn't make sense. Yet those of us committed to this practice had to contend with prejudice against staff perceived as junior. Until quite late in the twentieth century in some British companies there would be a managers' dining room and the workers' canteen – clear class division. I recall a senior manager responding to a presentation that I made that recommended involving operators in redesigning processes. He observed that it was 'like the tail wagging the dog'. At another presentation, a colleague had spelt 'continuous' wrong – he omitted the first 'u'. The same manager homed in on this typo and missed the point of the presentation. Over time, I won people over. I was also extremely fortunate to work with very bright and ambitious colleagues who equally wanted to make a difference as well. Paul Ferarrio was head of engineering, extremely smart and cooperative, and we formed a great partnership.

People start to deliver for you when you involve them. We developed new, team-based processes when operating a new production line, resulting ultimately in significant productivity improvements, including a 50 per cent reduction in turnover time. For example, in order to change a piece of equipment inside the production line, we designed bespoke pieces of equipment – a trolley at the exact height necessary and a sliding mechanism, used to slide the old tool out and the new one in. This replaced a system involving a crane that had been much more time-consuming. We also devised a more logical sequencing of products for the production line, which had the effect of reducing cleaning times. There was a reel of PVC that was used for coating, so Paul Ferarrio simply switched to a bigger roll, reducing the number of changeovers. Similarly, we increased the size of the bags that fed the raw material, constructing machinery to support them. There were major cost savings from having reduced maintenance time and more efficient use of the machinery, all the while maintaining the highest product quality. This type of leap forward in efficiency is only really possible by harnessing the contributions and enthusiasm of everyone in the team.

I was fortunate to have enlightened managers and fellow professionals: Our divisional manager, who gave us licence to experiment in teams if our changes improved quality, and Paul Ferarrio, our head of engineering. I caught up with Paul in 2020, in preparation for this book. He recalled my keenness on continuous improvement, saying: 'You got a guy in from the US to give us a pep talk, around 1988 or '89. To be honest, you seemed to get free rein, or between us we did. You were very much into Tom Peters ... how operators don't leave their brains at the door. We had a great time doing it ... they just let us get on with it. The fact that the organisation was quite small at Wellcome helped: only one site and we were in charge of our own destiny.'

We made significant progress through complexity reduction. In pharmaceuticals manufacture, the little strips with punched holes in which you find your tablets are known as 'blisters'. Over time, variations had proliferated such that there were ten different sizes. Progressively, we reduced the number of different blister sizes to just two, creating significant operational efficiency improvements and cost savings. This lesson in complexity reduction was to prove highly valuable throughout my career.

We kept asking: why? Why are we doing this? It is human nature to interrogate new proposals far more rigorously than existing procedures. Key to improvement is to interrogate everything, including the obvious, and to involve all relevant individuals in the discussion. Paul adds: 'It was about empowerment and team working. This was fundamental to the way we worked. If people aren't empowered, there's no point trying to effect change and get improvements. For the changeover, you just had to slide the piece out. Heavy pieces were hard to handle, but we made the trolley the right height. We colour coded the parts so they would fit and you could recognise them instantly. For one format there was a red dot, the corresponding position on the machine was also calibrated with a red dot. Engineers involved operators in the management of the line – they were doing the changeover. Before, engineers would have to come over.'

My supervisory and managerial roles at Wellcome formed the perfect grounding in key areas of operational management in a manufacturing industry. I had real-world lessons in matching supply and demand in a global business, balancing continuity of supply and resilience with efficiency and the need to prevent excessive inventory – in a highly specialised regulated manufacturing sector with one of the strictest quality regimes. It was tremendously satisfying to be able to implement my ideas on teamwork and management and see tangible positive results.

It wasn't until years later that I fully appreciated the grounding that Wellcome had instilled in me over the years – initially on work study and costings, later on processes and quality. Through the workplace studies, I learned how to calculate labour hours and machine hours to produce a fairly accurate operating cost for certain tasks. It transpired that this would be an immensely useful discipline later in my career, when I was responsible for global supply chain management. This learning enabled me both to identify smarter practices and justify them with data. Secondly, inventory management was very precise at Wellcome, as indeed in all pharmaceutical firms. The records and the inventory had to match exactly and we carried out random checks; the smallest discrepancy had to be reported and corrected, with lessons learned. Huge gains could be made from complexity reduction; life is complicated enough, so keep simple what you can keep simple. Also, there was people management: Wellcome gave me coaching in personal leadership skills, such as empathy, how to handle appraisals, communicate and motivate staff. Wellcome wasn't a business school, but it provided me with a first-rate, all-round education in management skills for a manufacturing firm. Much of the learning came from the teamwork and learning-by-doing, the constant experimentation and improvement, different disciplines cooperating, innovation and service delivery closely integrated.

Progress isn't always linear or continuous. Or guaranteed

A sad endnote to the case study of the production line improvements at Wellcome is that, after its takeover by the pharmaceutical giant Glaxo in 1995, the entire factory in Dartford was closed, with production moved to Glaxo sites. It was a sharp introduction to the concept of 'not invented here'.

Deliver What You Promise

The concepts of continual innovation, iteration and improvement are desirable, but never inevitable: they involve discipline and focus, and conscious agency. One of the most important lessons about management – indeed, about life – is that things can get worse instead of better! The case study in this chapter will be around 30 years old by the time people are reading it, but please do not assume that the lessons are therefore dated. We worked back from the needs of the customer, combining speed, efficiency and quality through a blend of teamwork and smart technology as part of a culture of commitment to continuous improvement. These principles are timeless.

I do not wish to be overly harsh in judgement of Glaxo's management at the time, because many of their people and processes were excellent. Indeed, it was during my time at Glaxo Wellcome that I first became acquainted with the phrase 'deliver what you promise'. And the takeover indirectly benefited me. There was a cull of Wellcome managers, but I was too junior to be affected and opportunities opened up for me within this multinational corporation. I formed a close working relationship with a Glaxo executive at the time. He encouraged me to volunteer for various projects. I applied for a promotion for which I thought I would stand little chance – yet I was appointed. This was an export role, which was a very different type of work. A big promotion, and my first global role, it was based at Glaxo's office in

Ware, Hertfordshire, to the north of London. It further added to my all-round grounding in business operations by exposing me to sales, shipping and distribution. My leader was supportive and very committed to coaching and growing people. Curiously, one of his initiatives led to my looking outside of the company. Through one of his contacts on the headhunting side, he arranged for me to undergo an assessment that included cognitive tests to identify aptitude and working styles. My assessor concluded that I had a strong entrepreneurial spirit and was likely to find a long career in a large corporation like Glaxo somewhat suffocating. I found this quite remarkable: Glaxo was paying someone to tell me I ought to consider leaving!

After another mega-merger, when Glaxo Wellcome became GlaxoSmithkline or GSK, in 2000, I found the office politics rather stressful and began to look for opportunities outside. It was then that I noticed a job advert for an intriguing role heading up operations and supply in North America for the legendary toy firm LEGO.

My career was heading for its biggest breakthrough yet.

Summary

The tremendous achievements, yet also frustrations, at Wellcome and later Glaxo Wellcome and GlaxoSmithkline, as a young manager, provided me with rich learning opportunities, both as observer and protagonist.

43

The 'not invented here' syndrome is real and its roots lie in very human characteristics: pride, ego and a sense of emotional ownership. Innovation and service delivery are not opposites, but rather they should be seen as closely linked. In a similar way, I have always found the distinction between supposedly 'hard' business concepts such as processes, finance and systems, contrasted with the 'soft' side of emotions and relationships, to be arbitrary and unhelpful. In the real world, all these dimensions are closely interlinked, as I shall discuss later in Chapter 12 (*see also* pages 193–201). This is linked to an understanding of the business as a complex, dynamic system rather than a set of assets and will be the subject of the next chapter.

Key principles from this chapter

- Innovation and execution are closely related, not inherent opposites. In many business contexts, it is too extreme to contrast 'disruption' with 'steady state' and more realistic to simultaneously consider what needs changing and what needs retaining.
- Disruption does not inevitably bring about improvement or even invention.
- Those involved in operations and service delivery can be, and need to be, as innovative as those in design or research and development.

Innovation is a Way of Thinking

- Innovation in business needs to be geared towards enhancing quality of life for the ultimate consumer, not change and disruption for its own sake.
- The most effective innovation often comes through continual improvement, which can create transformation through continuous iteration, rather than a one-off disruption.

How to implement the principles

- Try to review, at every meeting, how processes, services and products can be improved, as well as maintained.
- Conversely, if planning a major change initiative, play devil's advocate: will the change bring unintended consequences? Might existing services be interrupted or harmed? Ask yourself what needs to be nurtured and maintained.
- Change and innovation are always a means to an end: retain a consistent focus on impact on the ultimate consumers.

Chapter 3
A Business is a Living Organism

Around 2007, two years into my role as chief operations officer at LEGO, a friend of mine who was working at Procter & Gamble observed that he had never before encountered an operations executive with so much influence on strategy. I took this as a compliment, while acknowledging that it was also a result of circumstance: fixing key aspects of operations was central to the survival and turnaround at the company and I was closely associated with the reforms. It was also considered unusual for the head of a supply chain to hold regular meetings with retail customers, a practice I had begun in an earlier role in the North American operations.

To me, it has always been logical, and natural, to be enquiring about other aspects of the business, while of course respecting the domain knowledge of others. 'Deliver what you promise' is a maxim I learned early in my career. It is a timeless guide for everyone in management. Flowing naturally from this operating principle is the realisation that the whole enterprise must be engaged, that each must know what the other is doing so that the whole can be expertly choreographed. Affecting one part significantly will inevitably affect the whole.

Obvious? Seemingly not. I have learned in my career that when I have pursued an approach of close cooperation between different functions, of seeking to understand the perspective of internal and external stakeholders, I have often been going *against* conventional business logic. Rather than accept this, I started to question the basis of widely accepted operating assumptions.

Relatively early on in my career at LEGO, I was strongly influenced by the book *Execution: The Discipline of Getting Things Done* by Ram Charan and Larry Bossidy. The authors make a telling point that there is a difference between *leading* a business and *presiding* over it. Too many chief executives, they argue, fall into the latter category: they sit far above the operational reality. While it is necessary that they avoid becoming too immersed in the day-to-day business, and certainly one should not micro-manage, this point has often been over-interpreted. Chief executives should not be so distanced that they do not understand the operations. Delegating is obviously necessary, but they should know in depth the responsibilities and tasks that they are delegating, be confident that those responsible have the necessary skills and resources, and be able to handle informed questions about operational details. In *Execution*, the authors list example after example of chief executives skilled in strategic overview and financial analysis, wedded to their ambitious performance targets, but displaying a weak or superficial understanding of what their operational teams were actually doing, with disastrous results in every case.

I recall vividly the long flight from the US to Denmark, in 2004, when I read *Execution*. My usual routine with a night-time flight was to read for an hour or so, have a glass of wine, doze for a couple of hours, then wake up to skim through a few more pages. On this occasion I stayed awake the whole flight to finish the book – it was compelling. Yet while it articulated many features of my own approach to management uncannily well, it also raised deeper questions. Why were so many managers, appointed to the most senior executive posts, repeatedly making such basic errors by displaying a superficial understanding and lack of curiosity concerning the complex systems that they were in charge of? And why were so many boards making such unsuitable appointments? This seemed to point to some conceptual flaws within business education, in the preparation of executives and boards, and their understanding of their responsibilities. Those leaders who are merely presiding, rather than leading, just studying financial data, seemed to regard the organisation as a money-making machine that they oversee, rather than a complex organism that they directly affect. This misconception appeared to be linked to the view that it was eccentric for the head of one function to be knowledgeable about others.

Execution was first published in 2002, with a second edition in 2009, but it is still relevant today. Different studies have confirmed that the problems it discussed – lack of institutional knowledge and complex internal dynamics, emphasis upon setting targets and remaining above operational detail – remained a significant issue through the 2010s and into the 2020s. Indeed, the rise of artificial intelligence and the explosion in the amount of business intelligence available could increase the temptations to 'lead' by just studying the data, with limited knowledge of operations and how the different parts of the business work together.

An article in the May–June 2021 edition of the *Harvard Business Review* cited research showing a continued tendency among many boards to hire chief executives with little grasp of operational detail. The authors' study found that the failure to groom internal candidates, with deep institutional knowledge, for the CEO role was destroying hundreds of billions of dollars of value. Better succession planning would result in company valuations and investor returns that would be 20–25 per cent higher. In only 7.2 per cent of instances will an outside CEO hire have a 60 per cent chance of outperforming an insider. The authors cited separate research concluding that many company boards have 'an irrational bias toward exciting and unblemished external hires whom they know less about'.[4]

In a revealing interview in the *Financial Times* in February 2021, Jeff Immelt, former chief executive of the US-based conglomerate The General Electric Co. (GE), reflected on the difficulties of overseeing a complex company with interests that ran from turbines to financial services. His famous predecessor Jack Welch had built both scale and complexity to the group, which was an advantage in favourable market conditions, but resulted in a company almost impossible for an individual, or even a small executive team, fully to understand at an operational level. Immelt used the term 'The Blob' to express his difficulty in being able to have clear operational insight. The article observed: '"The Blob works until it doesn't," Immelt says, arguing that conglomerates can manage almost anything in favourable markets but that complexity becomes a liability when conditions turn. He still defends the logic of industrial conglomerates but says GE's former combination of industrial operations, financial services and the NBC media arm is "a bridge too far".'[5]

The different elements of a conglomerate may have different chief executives, strategies, services and markets, but they still interact with each other in complex and unpredictable ways. Obviously, the mutual impacts are even greater between different functions of the same unit or company.

Deliver What You Promise

Niels Duedahl, CEO of the Danish energy and telecoms group Norlys, said to me in an interview for this book in late 2020: 'You [Bali] taught me one thing that I never forgot: maybe it was Danish thinking that if you go down into the detail and the machine room, that was not so good for execs, you need to stay on high-level stuff. That was the recipe for the top leader . . . [but you] insisted that you have to know detail. I had thought that if you wanted to know detail, you would hire someone. I thought you were crazy to begin with, but 18 years later now, I can see clearly its importance. We have four leadership values [at Norlys]: one of them is to know the machine details. I can't stand leaders who are too conceptual, really despise that. Knowing the detail helps you gain the respect of people. You need to be able to engage in discussion at detail level . . . You need to quickly grasp the 20 per cent you need to know. Believing you can do it with two per cent – that's not possible.'

A survey in 2013 by the Economist Intelligence Unit, which I took part in, highlighted the finding that the difference between success and failure in business is often to be found in operations and in implementation. The report on the findings concluded that 'execution sets companies apart more than strategy formulation does, because fewer corporate leaders are as skilled at it.' The global survey of over 587 senior executives found a strikingly low success rate in terms of implementing strategy and an internal divide between those setting strategy and those implementing it. Companies with stronger ratings on C-suite involvement, good feedback mechanisms and better resourcing reported much stronger financial performance. The study also found that 61 per cent of respondents acknowledged difficulty in implementing strategies and only 56 per cent of strategic initiatives were successful. One problem was 'micro-management' by a C-suite executive, but a more serious and more common dysfunction was lack of buy-in from the senior level and disengagement between the C-suite and operations and project managers.

The researchers concluded: 'Rather than micromanaging, C-suite executives should identify and focus on the key initiatives and projects that are strategically relevant. Although the details of how to implement strategy vary significantly by company, survey respondents identify several areas where C-suite efforts are valuable. These include general oversight, leading and supporting strategic initiatives and communication. Top executives should also pay special attention to the key initiatives and projects that are most important to corporate strategy. This entails involving corporate leaders in high-level decisions on the selection and prioritisation of such initiatives as well as the allocation of resources to them – the core of strong project-portfolio management.'[6]

As with the findings from the *Execution* book a decade earlier, this points to some conceptual as well as operating errors. A business is a complex network of specialist teams of people. Every action has a reaction or reactions somewhere along the chain or in the system that may be positive or negative, intended or unexpected. At one level, this observation looks fairly obvious, but proper appreciation of this reality has been hampered by a flawed model of the company as a set of inert assets and departments. Such an inanimate model has tended to encourage fiefdoms and discourage an understanding of how the interconnected whole functions. There is a connected conceptual error, which is the separation of 'hard' and 'soft' business matters, which I shall discuss more fully in Chapter 12 (*see also* pages 193–201). This division is illogical, everything is interconnected. The chief executive's psychology and demeanour will affect performance more than the last quarter's financial figures, and performance and culture are part of the same whole. Indeed, an insight from the granular detail of Ram Charan and Larry Bossidy's descriptions in their book, *Execution*, is how the highly effective leaders balance support and challenge in the way in which they hold performance conversations with their direct reports. They are nurturing a healthy culture, not merely demanding that targets get met. The 'hard' and 'soft' approaches are fused into a coherent whole, not arbitrarily segregated.

At times in my career I have been accused of micromanaging – perhaps sometimes the accusation was fair, but undoubtedly sometimes it was not. It arose because I would often ask detailed questions to satisfy myself that an issue was being properly addressed – that may have been to do with quality or packing or other issues. I wasn't trying to tell people how to do their job, I was being intellectually curious: if something didn't seem quite right, I would enquire. I'm not perfect, and perhaps I asked one or two questions too many on occasion, but it was never with the intention of micro-managing. I took advice from my mentor at the time to reassure myself on this point.

When I joined LEGO, in the early 2000s, the supply chain was a mess. It was also being scapegoated by the wider organisation – given the almost unbelievably pejorative nickname of 'Assholes INC'. These were symptoms of a seriously ill organisation. I had to fix the supply chain, to be sure, and I had the relevant experience to begin that task. But there was a wider challenge: to encourage cross-disciplinary collaboration, to foster a culture of accountability which included putting tough questions to other functions as well as supply. There appeared to be limited wider understanding of the enterprise as an integrated whole – at least before Jørgen Vig Knudstorp began to get a grip on strategy and operations in the mid-2000s after his appointment as CEO.

Departmental rivalry was so pronounced it was severely hampering our ability to deliver what we promised; this was the challenge for the supply chain. But there were also serious problems in being able to promise what the market actually wanted. Dysfunctions were observable across design, marketing, supply and strategy.

Think deeply, think clearly

My experience at LEGO threw up conceptual as well as practical issues for me, and not for the first time in my career. In earlier roles, working primarily in the pharmaceuticals sector, I witnessed practices that struck me as illogical; not only that, but they were repeated despite evidence of failure or, at best, sub-optimal outcomes. Habitual, repeated errors seem to point to flawed thinking and operating models.

We get into a practical mess if we are not thinking clearly. If we don't have a clear and accurate understanding of what the organisation *is*, we are in a poor place to improve its direction and performance. The purpose of this chapter is to drum home the message: the organisation is *not* a collection of inert assets and departments, it is a living organism – dynamic and productive if well-led and managed; dysfunctional and sick if not. You may need to outsource some functions, you may be more expert in some specialisms that are critical to competitive advantage than in others, but it is always an interconnected whole. If you must use metaphors, better to use organic ones like organism and sickness than inanimate ones like structure.

A Business is a Living Organism

Management is difficult. Sometimes, in the real unpredictable world, there are difficult trade-offs. Real businesses and real life are full of unanticipated hazards; you often lack time to discover all the data and evidence you would like before making a decision and so it is easy to be guided by heuristics and familiar strategies. Given this, it is all the more important to have a clear understanding of the reality of the organisation and of the task. The difficulties in implementing the principles of the quality movement, as discussed in Chapter 2 (*see also* pages 35–41), arose because some good ideas were thwarted by the departmentalisation of the twentieth-century company, with an excessive emphasis on specialisation and separation, underplaying or even denying the reality of interconnectedness and the importance of human connection.

Around 20 years ago, as I began my career at LEGO, I found separation and conflict between different functions amid a full-blown crisis, yet this was a company with excellent products and highly talented and motivated people. The story of how we turned things around provides much of the case study material for this book. I know from my current coaching work that such challenges have remained only too prevalent in the business world, but for the next history lesson, we go back to the period 2002–03, as I began my role as head of packing for LEGO North America.

Lesson from LEGO

'You've never been trained in it?' I asked the operator on the production line at LEGO. I was holding the quality operating manual open at the page showing the process that I had been referring to. The machinery was whirring in the background, we had to raise our voices slightly to be heard. There was a row of 12–14 vibratory bowls, each about 1m wide, in which LEGO bricks were automatically sorted and counted, then dropped into bags.

'No,' came the reply.

I took the manual to the supervisor, who told me: 'I've never even seen it before.'

The official LEGO quality operating processes looked impressive on paper; the problem was that operators did not follow them – or were not even aware of them, in some cases. This was not the only concern as I began my role as head of packing for LEGO, in October 2002 at the site in Enfield, Connecticut, which is in eastern US, about half-way between Boston and New York. I had been informed that the company operated a system known as MRP-II, or Materials Requirement Planning (sometimes known as Manufacturing Resources Planning). This is a standard integrated information system used to support manufac-turing processes, but I discovered that the system was not true MRP-II – it was a bespoke approach that required much tacit knowledge. Warehousing and stock-keeping were a bit of a mess. We would have a meeting at 8am, we would discuss the orders that had come in and would have to be packed – but by 12 it was discovered that we couldn't because a part was missing. The quality of manufacture was always faultless – please don't be concerned if you still have LEGO bricks manufactured in this period! – but there were sometimes problems in the packing. An error that occurred from time to time was in a symmetrical model such as a *Star Wars* spaceship: instead of left and right versions of a piece, there would be two lefts or two rights. A focus on efficiency and productivity, supported by incentives for targets on 'bricks per hour', needed correcting.

During this period, I became seen as something of a nuisance because I would stop the machines to check for quality and accuracy. Incorrectly packed boxes would be put on the stop list; when I started at Enfield, they were allowed to stay there for too long – I wanted the period brought down to 24 hours. We began to put the emphasis on correcting errors quickly, learning from those errors, putting the appropriate remedies in place and not allowing matters to drift.

My approach to these matters was an example of my grounding at the pharmaceutical company Wellcome in England in the 1980s. The inventory management that I learned there was about precision and I saw no reason why LEGO would not benefit from a similarly disciplined approach. Errors such as the left-right component problem should never happen – imagine the frustration and disappointment for a child a day or two after opening a *Star Wars* gift at Christmas or a birthday, only to discover there were parts missing! I was to have zero tolerance of that type of error. A colleague came up with a simple solution for symmetrical models – of simply reserving designated vibrating bowls for respectively left- and right-sided pieces. We brought the error rate of this problem down to zero within 18 months.

I understood costings well, thanks to my thorough grounding at Wellcome, but the costings system at LEGO was opaque and unusable. There was something called the 'Net Production Price'. Throughout my 16 years with the company I never had a full or satisfactory explanation of its calculation. Costs seemed to be added and taken away arbitrarily. I knew from my experience at Wellcome that greater precision was perfectly possible.

Errors were frustrating because manufacturing and packing LEGO components were not the most complex processes. The bricks have a long shelf life, temperature control is not such a critical issue and maintaining high quality standards should not have been a big deal. I could perceive a problem that is common to many workplaces: over-complicating processes. One of the points I would make in my early years was: 'Our process is simple. We take granular feed material, we melt it into plastic, we mould it into bricks and other pieces, these get packed and sent to stores.'

Keeping things simple in business, I discovered, is rarely simple. But it is an essential discipline.

At the Enfield site, there was a manufacturing plant and a sales and operations office on the same campus, but relations between the two departments were not good. And then there was Billund. This is the name of the town in Denmark where LEGO was founded and hosts its headquarters. When I started in Enfield, the term 'Billund' had acquired the personality of an overseer or even an ogre; a quasi-parental but vaguely threatening presence that hovered above us. 'Billund won't let us do that,' I would hear. Or: 'Billund decided.' I adopted friendly sarcasm by way of reply: 'What, the whole town? The mayor? Did they hold a vote?' More seriously, I would ask for details: precisely what can we do and what can't we? There was a lack of a sense of agency or autonomy on our site. I decided that no one would get into trouble for raising quality standards and I insisted that we take more control over our own operations. The team I was working with were exceptionally bright and I took to the culture and the products; I had little doubt that they were capable of the improvements that I could see were needed. Some things needed to change radically and, as we learned of deteriorating financial figures a few months into my tenure, quite rapidly also. But how could I go about this? How could I tell my team, gently, that their operational standards were not world-class, in the way that they had imagined?

In the end, I didn't go down the 'gentle' route, the problem was too serious for that. I would have to ensure their engagement, but that wasn't going to be achieved by lacking candour. I would back my team, I would defend their interests against others, but we had to up our performance first – that was going to be the deal.

I instituted weekly meetings with my direct reports. For me, regular meetings were to check on performance and to ensure accountability. It turned out that this represented something of a culture change. A big moment occurred at a meeting relatively early in my tenure. There was a quality issue and the previous meeting had assigned an action to a manager – fairly senior in the team – to be completed by the following week. Next week came and we started the meeting. The action hadn't been completed. I asked him why. He wasn't able to give an explanation. I said sorry, this is not acceptable. I asked him to leave the meeting immediately, work on the action and report to me first thing the next day.

The room went silent. I am not sure I would have produced more shock if I had taken out a revolver and shot someone. The people are not with me, I sensed. I would address this issue, but first things first, there was a point to make. After the meeting one of the guys came to me and said: 'Bali, since you joined you have said we should be honest. Well, I have a piece of feedback for you: the way you treated the manager is not a LEGO way of doing things.'

I respected his honesty in telling me this directly, but decided to hold my ground. Ensuring accountability is the right thing to do. The following day, I spoke with him and told him this. 'Oh,' he replied. 'We are going to be in for some interesting times!'

My team were terrific people in terms of commitment and ability; the weaknesses lay in the processes and associated execution. Once these were improved I knew the performance we were capable of would be tremendous. The LEGO brand and products evoke tremendous enthusiasm and affection, and I admired the capability and allegiance of the staff, their commitment, loyalty, wanting to do the right thing. I did not have to work to encourage them to turn the company around, they were inspired to do so – it was a question of how. In the period of crisis, 2002–04, some colleagues left, but many decided to stay and they inspired me.

Winning the team over

One of the many benefits of being honest and insisting on accountability is that you earn respect – as long as you are consistent. I was with my team and I was equally strict on behalf of them if I felt that they were being treated unfairly by other departments. Early in 2003 an opportunity arose both to spread the culture of accountability on the Enfield site and to win over the hearts and minds of my team.

LEGO had done a deal with the NBA, the National Basketball Association, linked to a LEGO toy featuring a basketball court and mini figures as players. There was a campaign that the marketing team were heavily promoting. Those of us in operations knew about the initiative, but we hadn't been adequately consulted. Unexpectedly, I took a call from a manager at the warehouse. He said, 'It's full, full of basketballs.' I walked over to the warehouse. There were pallets, six-high and 20 metres long. Corridors were full as well. Basketballs, fully inflated – there was a quip about them being filled 'with Chinese air – can't we have American air?' – in their square cardboard boxes, direct from the manufacturer; basketballs everywhere. A LEGO marketing manager had placed an order with a factory in China as part of the offer, but he didn't have authority for that. The problem had been dumped upon us to deal with – and it was a major problem, because we had no space for other products. Factories would have to come to a standstill. I was devastated.

As the senior manager on the spot, I needed to do something so to begin with I phoned the marketing manager who had made the order. He had secured a good deal. The price was good and the numbers were right to support the offer but delivery should have been phased and other key partners in the business informed. He told me: 'It's not my problem.'

On hearing this, I decided to make it his problem so I started moving the basketballs outdoors, into the parking lot. I called him back to inform him: 'There is no security. Plus, if it rains, the packaging will disintegrate. I'm doing it.'

I called some of my team to help me. We put the basketballs outside, physically, one by one.

The rest of the organisation descended on me. This action caused outrage, but I stood my ground. My case was clear and I clearly articulated it: 'We have to have accountability and authority in the right place, and we have to have everyone abide by the rules. Doing the right thing in the wrong way is still wrong and we cannot tolerate that, certainly not on a regular basis. A marketing manager cannot make an order.'

So, we agreed a process. To deal with the immediate problem, we brought the basketballs back in, initially back into the warehouse, but then rented 40-ft storage containers and stored the basketballs in them, while to prevent a recurrence, my counterparts in other departments agreed to stick with agreed protocols for purchasing.

While the stand that I took was primarily around processes and accountability, and managing relationships between departments, a benign unintended consequence was that my team admired me for it. They felt someone was looking out for their interests, they rallied around me – it had been such a visible and public gesture that I was on their side.

There was a key incident. At LEGO there were frequent new product lines. At the end of each order, you had to reconcile – check that the packing is correct and hence that the inventory records are accurate and that the customer will get what they asked for. Simple maths but an important discipline, with an impact upstream and downstream. We were just finishing packing a *Star Wars* item when some of the marketing guys came down and took some boxes off the line. They wanted samples to show customers and they picked up 20 boxes and took them away. This threw our inventory data out, which was particularly exasperating for me, because I was putting so much effort into improving inventory management and data, and instilling these disciplines into my team. Moreover, unauthorised removal of boxes would directly affect the bonuses of people on my team as they were linked to inventory management. I thought that this was unacceptable.

'The next time it happens, call me. I will come down,' I told my team members.

A Business is a Living Organism

In those days we used to have pagers. A few days later, my pager bleeped. I finished my meeting, went down. My colleague told me: 'They've taken ten boxes. I tried to stop him, but he wouldn't listen.'

So, I told my colleague: 'Do you want to have some fun? Come with me, get an operator to come along.'

We went along to the marketing department, which was in a separate building on the same site. The office door was shut, but I knocked and we went in. The marketing manager was hosting a meeting, people sat at a desk with merchandise in piles and on shelves around them. The look on his face was one close to horror. I said to my colleague: 'Take any boxes you want.' We took six boxes – we didn't say anything, just walked out with them.

Of course, before too long I received a call from the marketing manager's boss. I simply explained what was happening – also, that I had notified them that they shouldn't be taking boxes, as it disrupted inventory management and order closure, meant that reconciliation was not adding up and affected bonuses. The practice of marketing folk letting themselves into our shop floor and removing items promptly ceased.

With these confrontations, I was not seeking to nurture inter-departmental tension or rivalry. It was a case of assertiveness, not a turf war – though I recognise there is the risk of that if you become *too* assertive. I strongly believe in partnership, but it has to be a partnership of equals and respect. Being called 'Assholes INC' in operations, and having people wade into our space and take stuff, showed a lack of respect. My staff loved me for taking this stand and, in due course, we established a strong partnership and good rapport with our colleagues in marketing. This type of negotiation is similar to the transactional relationship with customers such as retailers, which I will discuss later in Chapter 10 (*see also* page 176). Their interests overlap strongly, but they are not the same. Standing up for yourself is not hostility – although of course a sensible balance has to be struck!

One of my American staff members at Enfield put it well when he made a speech at a staff meeting during this period, directed at his colleagues. He stood up and said: 'Look, Bali is our quarterback, we have to defend him. If we deliver what we say, that's how we support him. He will do everything for you.'

Summary

In 2003 LEGO was a very sick being and that sickness was in just about every discipline, yet there were still some brilliant people, fantastic products and a large international fanbase. Clearly, some things had gone very seriously awry and equally clearly, there remained much potential for a turnaround programme. The theme of this chapter is that the company is like an organism. This is a more accurate imagery than that of a structure, but it does have to be used with care. It does not mean that a nurturing approach is uniformly correct. You will see from the case study that there is at least as much emphasis on challenging people and holding them to account as there is on support and creating psychological safety. It means collaboration between functions – but collaboration based on mutual respect, which may require assertiveness to maintain.

A business exists primarily to deliver a service or product to the consumer. During the crisis at LEGO we were failing on many measures, in different functions, so the whole had to be reformed for recovery to be possible. Hence, those of us in supply became equal partners. We showed that this is as necessary for strategic renewal (the subject of Chapter 5, *see also* pages 89–114), as for delivering what we promise.

Key principles from this chapter

- A business is always a complex, interconnected organism, not an inert set of departments. Every action has reactions that are felt somewhere in the system, including those that are unexpected.
- There is a difference between leading a business and presiding over it. C-suite executives need to avoid becoming so preoccupied by day-to-day matters that they lose sight of the big picture – but a more common problem

is that they lack adequate knowledge of the operational reality and that the business, or a part of it, becomes 'The Blob', in the words of ex-GE chief executive Jeff Immelt.

- Execution sets companies apart more than strategy formulation does, because fewer corporate leaders are as skilled at it.

- All functions within the business directly affect the whole.

- Outsourced suppliers and partners effectively form part of a wider ecosystem – you cannot outsource responsibility.

- There needs to be healthy collaboration between all key parts of the system. This means honest, in-depth conversations and permission to disagree while treating others with respect.

How to implement the principles

- A senior executive needs to ask detailed questions of operational heads, to ensure a good overview of the functioning of the business; those areas that are performing well, in addition to those presenting problems. The questions need to cover both the what (data, quantitative information) and the why (what are the root causes?).

- Presenting problems must always be addressed by looking at the whole system, in addition to the individual person or department, in order to prevent scapegoating, or other forms of unfair or limited types of understanding and judgement.

- All functions operate in collaboration with one another and a failure that emerges in one part of the system may have contributing dysfunctions in another part. For example, a design may be unpopular because of inadequate market research, rather than lack of ability for the design team; quality problems in manufacture may be due to skills gaps, faults in manufacture or low-quality raw materials, or a combination.

- Balance support with accountability. In their conversations with departmental heads and other key line managers, executives need to be rigorous in setting standards, but also responsible in ensuring psychological safety and that employees have sufficient information and resources.

Chapter 4
Personal Resilience

Early in my managerial career at the pharmaceutical company Wellcome, I was unsuccessful in an application for a promotion for which I had been confident and hopeful. For a while I felt very despondent. I feel that I managed to avoid any drop in my performance at work, but I was drawn to the company of others who had been passed over for promotion and who had come to feel somewhat jaundiced about the company and their prospects. A common refrain was: 'It's not fair.' For a while when you are feeling hurt, receiving sympathy and sharing grievances can be soothing, almost enjoyable, but only for a while. I began to perceive a danger. As humans, we tend to move in the direction of our recurring thoughts and conversations. I realised that if the narratives I was most exposed to were to do with setbacks, excuses and blaming others, and if I socialised with people who had given up on ambition, I was likely to hold myself back so I made a conscious decision to change my socialising patterns and to begin to rediscover my ambition.

Personal resilience is a combination of building on your inner strengths, making good decisions and learning from bad ones – or at least, ones that didn't work out. One of the paradoxical benefits of having to overcome poverty and discrimination is that you do tend to be adaptable and you develop the capability to overcome unwelcome events. A view that I have come across in some people is the expectation that social and economic life can – or indeed *should* – be benign, stable and predictable for decades on end. This is an unrealistic expectation. In 2020, during the Covid-19 pandemic, some commentators described the year as exceptionally dreadful and yearned for a return to 'normal'. But disruption *is* normal. Unfortunately, tragedy, unexpected events such as pandemics, recessions and wars, are all part of life, and 2020 was probably not the most disrupted or unpredictable year in modern history.

During my time at Wellcome, it was affected by the takeover by the UK giant Glaxo. As described earlier in Chapter 2 (*see also* pages 41–2), this was a hugely disruptive affair. Some of the managers who had spent their careers at Wellcome had expected this paternalistic company to remain in the same ownership and continue in the same uninterrupted stable way of working for the remainder of their working lives and beyond so they could not cope with the takeover and its drastic impact. I acknowledge that some of the measures taken by the incoming Glaxo managers were overly sweeping, even harsh, but it was notable that some of those made redundant regarded their working lives as over and never looked for another opportunity. I found this to be profoundly sad.

My ambitions when young were vague and unshaped. I certainly didn't tell a careers adviser that I planned to be a leading executive at the firm that made LEGO – something I didn't even play with as a child! Perhaps it was better that way. When I have encountered MBA graduates with a rigid plan to be line manager by a certain age, vice president some years later, CEO by their mid-40s, specifying which sector, I wince a little and fear the young individual is unprepared for life's unplanned events. It's perfectly laudable to be ambitious, but also to build in a little flexibility and adaptability in case Plan A gets knocked off the desired course – which almost always occurs.

I have sometimes been asked where my social, and business, confidence came from. But I am unable to offer a definitive answer; it has always just been there. As a boy and young man growing up in Kent in the 1960s and 1970s, social integration was an uneven affair, punctuated by anxiety, but I recall being able to confront my fears and push at boundaries. I had a close family and made some friends, although at times I felt lonely and homesick for India. As noted earlier, on occasion I received the most appalling racist abuse. As I got older and my friends and I started going out in an evening, I overheard rumours that there were some pubs in the town who would refuse to serve Asians. I would feel panic rising in my chest as we made our way to a hostelry, my heart racing with anxiety, although it never actually happened that we were barred from entering. Curiously, my confidence seemed to grow as a result; there was a sense of being able to overcome barriers, to be accepted in places where I had been warned I wouldn't be. I have a tendency that, if someone says 'You can't do that', I am likely to see it as a challenge that I wish to rise to, so while many experiences in my teenage years were emotionally uncomfortable, by overcoming hardship and prejudice one can gain resilience and independence of mind; moreover, my family were tremendously supportive. For all the challenges and struggles, I did not wish to return to India. I felt I could make it in this society. I was also tremendously fortunate in finding the love of my life at an early age. Sati and I met, fell in love and married; we are still together today, with two grown-up children.

Some of the teachers at the Gordon School, which I attended, were encouraging and the headteacher was kind and quite influential. A most significant event occurred when he gave me a lift in his E-type Jaguar. The way it came about was that the teachers' cricket team were lacking a player for a match, an away fixture at St George's School on the other side of town, and it was suggested that I make up the numbers. My headmaster learned of my selection and asked me as he passed in the corridor: 'But how are you going to get there?' 'I don't know,' I replied. 'I shall give you a lift then,' he replied. That suited me. The drive to St George's was only a two- to three-mile trip across town, no country road, no chance to get up to any speed. I stepped into this classic high-performance two-seater sports car, pale metallic blue paint glinting in the sun, sank into the leather passenger seat and heard the throaty petrol roar of the engine as it was fired up. For a boy, this was thrilling; it was an exciting fantasy to imagine I might own an E-type Jaguar one day (which I finally do – I am the third owner of a 1967 vintage E-type, in excellent condition, the same colour, housed in a garage I had constructed to the front of my house for the purpose). So when a careers adviser at school suggested that I become a plumber, I was silently defiant. No offence to plumbers, who do a skilled and important job, but I began nurturing different ambitions, though not fully articulated at this stage. As noted, I did not have a defined career plan in mind; a specific goal to be CEO of this type of company or a start-up entrepreneur of something else. It was more a step-by-step ambition: to make something of myself and to make the most of the opportunities that presented themselves to me as they arose.

At the time, in the 1970s, there was no sixth form at the Gordon School and the expectation was that you left at 16 after sitting what were known as CSEs. The English exam system back then was two-tier: those considered more academic sat O-levels, the rest of us CSEs. My recollection is that only a small proportion of the school population went on to study A-levels and graduate at 18; an even smaller proportion went to university. This is confirmed by historical data, which showed that the proportion of schoolchildren achieving three or more A-level passes was just 6 per cent in the mid-1970s, rising to over 20 per cent by the start of the millennium. There was a similar trend with attendance at university.[7] I wished to further my education and so I attended the Springhead technical school in nearby Northfleet to sit my O-levels but, realising that A-levels would take a further two years' study, I instead left at age 17 to take up paid employment, initially as a production line attendant at AEI cable factory in Northfleet. Later, I secured a similar role at the pharmaceutical firm Wellcome, which led to the opportunity to gain my first promotion to a managerial role (*see also* Chapter 2, page 34).

You are responsible for your learning

Perhaps the single most important piece of advice I gave my children as they were growing up, and that I offer in this chapter, is to treat every day as a learning opportunity. Don't make assumptions and check the beliefs of yourself or others against the actual evidence. Keep an enquiring mind. Don't assume that a convenient soundbite tells an accurate story and always recognise that you have more to learn. A comment I have heard from individuals who feel frustrated at work is: 'I've been in this role two/three years and I haven't learned anything. They haven't provided any courses.' I find that an extraordinary viewpoint – it's *your* responsibility to be continually learning. There were two glaring issues that struck me when I heard such sentiments: firstly, you can always book your own course, or buy the textbooks. More fundamentally, however, every day in your working life offers opportunities for learning; for seeing how services can be improved, or your information enriched, or your skills enhanced. Life itself is a rich college of learning and effective managers see their role as one of continual improvement. One may go to college and get a first-class degree, but that doesn't guarantee common sense. In business leadership roles, strategy is best understood as a process of enquiry and discovery, as will be discussed in Chapter 5 (*see also* pages 89–114). An approach of passive expectation of 'learning opportunities' to be granted from on high by a benevolent force is unrealistic and self-defeating.

My family's entrepreneurial spirit was strong, yet I have to acknowledge that, as a young adult, I was not a successful entrepreneur – at least, I was not successful financially, although the experience was educational. My wife Sati and I are both from business-owning families; my family was in retail, Sati's was in the garment trade. I saw an opportunity to build my own business, starting with a market stall selling clothing. There were low-entry requirements in terms of capital investment: the main outlay was for the physical rails, tarpaulin and a vehicle. As it was family, the inventory was on credit, and I paid them as I sold, so I bought a van and began trading.

To begin with, we had traded on the weekend, but as I aspired to be an entrepreneur we decided I should leave my day job and seek to build a business by starting as a full-time market trader. I discovered, however, that the profit margins were thin and it was tough. Rainy or cold days were miserable, we were unable to gain a stall on the busier and more in-demand markets in Dartford and Gravesend, so had to drive to different parts of the county, to towns such as Faversham and Margate, where there would be fewer customers. Sometimes, you would spend £8 on petrol, pay £10 for your pitch and your day's takings were just £10. This was no business to be in. I also learnt that over-reliance on a single supplier can be damaging to you.

This failure to make a success as a market trader was disappointing, but I do not recall feeling crushed. I was young, still confident about my abilities and I took a pragmatic view. Every failure is an opportunity to learn and if you stop learning, you die. I have learned through life, as I acknowledge many others have learned, that it is a mistake to become overly exuberant with success or overly despondent after a setback. At this time in my life, in any case, there was not the time nor the opportunity to wallow in self-pity: we had started a family and I began to reconsider my entrepreneurial ambitions and opt instead for qualifications and a profession.

Early in my career at Wellcome, and while our son was still young, we tried again as retailers. Sati and I set up a shop selling handbags and luggage, next door to the family grocery store in the High Street. Having given up full-time work on becoming a mother, she was able to combine running the shop with childcare. It wasn't a success, however, and we closed after just over a year. I learned an important lesson: that cash is king. We had taken out a second mortgage on the house to set up the business and the debt caused us problems. Never again would I use debt to finance an enterprise with an element of risk. I decided to re-double my efforts to secure advancement through qualifications and a profession but there was no need to quell my enquiring mind and innovative ideas, I simply brought them to my new workplaces and ultimately, they helped the business and helped me gain promotion.

I also decided that, having left school at age 17 with a few exam passes, I needed to study for qualifications and so I enrolled in evening classes, studying business management, first for a Higher National Certificate (HNC) and later a degree from South Bank University in London. Wellcome generously helped contribute to the costs of my study and I applied for, and was accepted, my first managerial role.

Before promotion to management, I had begun driving taxis in the evenings and at weekends to keep the family solvent. Among taxi drivers, I would come across the same slightly mocking attitude towards learning that I had experienced with some fellow pupils. While waiting for my next customer, I would be reading Tom Peters, Charles Handy or some other management author. This would prompt gentle ridicule from some of the other drivers. In a similar way, at school I had been astonished to come across an anti-learning attitude among some pupils, for whom being studious was seen as being geeky or uncool. I never understood the mindset that intellectual curiosity or ambition were matters to provoke shame and I dealt robustly with the attitude by ignoring it, while wondering also if there might be an opportunity later in life to demonstrate to my erstwhile colleagues the long-term benefits of study.

Subtle racism is still racism

Some of my experiences of being almost always the only Asian or black person in a team have been challenging. One will occasionally hear disparaging or discriminatory comments and there is the almost continuous stress of making a judgement on whether to confront them or stay silent. If you say nothing, the unfairness can continue to build, undermining a culture of fairness and meritocracy; if you do challenge attitudes, you can be seen as a radical or a victim. It is almost impossible to get this balance right and a sense of frustration builds up, resulting in an accumulation of internalised anxiety over the years.

Even among some quite liberal commentators in the media, one can come across a biased framing of the issue, in which a degree of endemic prejudice against persons of colour is regarded as normal and those who protest against it are seen as political radicals or trouble-makers. This is an irrational and prejudiced framing: we should see equality as normal and prejudice as an unacceptable and politically extreme position – even if it is subtle and indirect. There is still much progress to be made in this direction.

On one occasion at LEGO, I reported back to my team in the US. One female colleague asked me how many women managers had been at the meeting. I replied that there had been four or five and then questioned her, asking why it was never an issue that I was the only non-white person at this and many other management meetings. Raising the issue of female representation is perfectly correct, of course, but for me this was yet another occasion on which it was clear that people within the organisation cared about some forms of representation but were blind to others.

One of the more effective interventions on this issue came while I was still at school. There was a painful encounter, when one of my friends made a disparaging comment about Asian immigrants, then turned to me and said: 'But you're different, Bali.' I replied that this comment was exceptionally offensive. To his credit, he apologised. And to his even greater credit, he sought me out some weeks later to apologise again. Much less forgivable was when I heard similar sentiments, years later, from educated managers at a pharmaceutical company, with less awareness or remorse. Nearly half a century on, this kind of polite, rational challenging of prejudiced views is still necessary.

Asking for help is not a weakness

Resilience and confidence are necessary attributes in a manager and there is a balance to be struck to avoid becoming over-confident, which can lead to serious misjudgements. Being confident of your knowledge in a healthy way means being aware of the limits of your knowledge. Striking the right balance between confidence and humility is a daily challenge for a manager. Those who assume that they are always right create obvious risks around hubris and over-confidence bias. Being too deferent and indecisive creates different risks: potentially tolerating weak performance and weakening accountability. I have sought to be decisive where I am confident that the data and evidence support my view, supported by insights derived from experience. Where I need more information, I have no hesitation in asking someone, to acknowledge that I need advice. I've never had a problem saying I don't know something – not asking for help is a hidden weakness.

Summary

My early life was very different to that of most people I have worked with. There may, nonetheless, be lessons from this chapter for managers of any background. Some challenges are common to all aspiring executives in the same way that many of the managerial disciplines discussed in this book are universal and timeless. Everyone will benefit from taking responsibility for their own education, finding the right balance between confidence and humility, asking the right questions, displaying resilience in response to setback or tragedy and staying grounded when experiencing success. Everyone's experience is different; everyone will have their own inner strengths and it is helpful to become self-aware around strengths and weaknesses. Personal resilience cannot be taught, unlike accountancy or engineering; it is a quality to be nurtured as part of the lived experience. This is not to say, however, that you cannot become better at it.

Key principles from this chapter

- Every day is a learning opportunity.
- We tend to follow the world of our internal narratives, so if yours includes one of feeling sorry for yourself, you will hold yourself back and probably find yourself socialising with others equally held back by self-pity and grievance.
- Knowing the limits of your knowledge is a key asset, together with knowing when and where to ask for help.
- Learning is primarily the individual's responsibility.
- If you experience prejudice, it is justifiable and often necessary to challenge this appropriately.
- Those who have experienced prejudice or economic hardship, or both, may have a hidden advantage in being more prepared for unpleasant shocks and better equipped to respond to them than those who have had a more sheltered upbringing.

How to implement the principles

- After a major setback it helps to acknowledge the pain, which may be one of loss, or even humiliation or trauma. In addition, set aside time to reflect rationally and ask yourself: What have I learned? How much was the event a consequence of my decisions? What can I do differently in the future?

Personal Resilience

- For individuals of colour in a white Western business world, there is no easy guide on when and how to confront prejudice. It helps to challenge politely and rationally, encouraging the individual to learn. This is not always possible, but you can secure some unlikely little victories.
- Maintaining an enquiring mind is invaluable: always challenge assumptions, check against evidence. This attribute is key simultaneously to personal resilience and effectiveness as a manager.
- Seize opportunities. In particular, seek out opportunities to learn, rather than waiting for training to be offered as a gift or a perk.

Chapter 5
Strategy is a Process of Discovery

It is almost certainly the case that most people who graduate from a business school want to work on strategy and equally true that only a minority get to do so. Strategy is sexy, it's cool, it's fun. We get to shape the future. Whose ego is not flattered by the opportunity? If you put the term 'business strategy' into the search function on the Amazon Kindle books section, it currently yields 400 pages of results.

Yet while smart strategy is essential for business success, it is not sufficient. Plenty of businesses have a superbly thought-through and coherent strategy, well suited for the context, yet still fail. Throughout my career I encountered a prejudice in which strategy is venerated, and operations is regarded as junior, even as 'dirty'. The bias is deeply ingrained. For example, early in my career at LEGO, I renamed a meeting from 'operations update' to 'strategic update' and noticed a sharp increase in attendance from senior individuals, even though the format and agenda remained unchanged. Perhaps the attitude even has its origin in the feudal system; there is a natural preference to be in the manor house devising plans rather than to be out toiling in the fields. In an advanced economy with high levels of skills, knowledge and cooperation required throughout the enterprise, such a division is a severely limiting anachronism.

There are prices to pay for fetishising the development of business strategy: one is to downplay the importance of operations and delivery – a very serious problem. Another is that, with the clamour and collective desire to shape strategy by business-school graduates, personal desire and ego can distort an honest and responsible approach. For all that business students adore strategy, read about it and study it, ironically it has been one of the most frequently misunderstood aspects of business analysis that I have encountered among managers in my long career. There are two common misconceived approaches, based in part on misconceptions: one is to veer too much towards autocracy and secrecy; the other is the opposite tendency, to be overly democratic and uncontrolled, permitting every function to have its own strategy.

In a real, living, adaptable business, you do need a clear strategy and a single strategy, but it is not a fixed template devised in secret by an elite cabal. It is more a continual dialogue between the senior team, the rest of the organisation and, more importantly still, customers and the rest of the outside world. There is an emerging consensus around an

approach to strategy that is an ongoing process of experimentation, iteration and adaptation, but it has taken a long
time to develop. In this chapter I will articulate this philoso-
phy, based on a blend of personal experience and insights
from leading intellectuals. It is necessary also to discuss some
misconceptions that have slowed the progress of this more
enlightened approach, namely the 'strategy-as-a-rigid-plan'
myth and the 'everyone-must-have-a-strategy' myth.

The 'strategy-as-a-rigid-plan' myth

Strategy can be misunderstood as a rigid plan, devised by a
small cadre of senior leaders and then implemented throughout the organisation in a top-down approach. It is assumed
that implementation is a one-way exercise in communication, often described with a metaphor: either of the roll-out,
or of the cascade. In benign and stable conditions, with fairly
predictable market conditions, such an approach may be
effective, but those situations can never be guaranteed and
are probably becoming increasingly rare in an age of rapid
technological development and political instability. This type
of context may appear in an MBA lecture hall, but not in the
turbulent, political and unstable real world outside.

My understanding of the company as being like an
organism is an analogy that was revived for me in a conversation with Dr Jules Goddard of the London Business
School in preparation for this book. He described how a

healthy organisation evolves. Too much business change involves changing too much, being dazzled by that which is new. While failing to renew and adapt can be fatal for a business, change has to be optimal and focused upon that which helps survival and growth. Evolution operates through continual renewal, experimentation and adaptation, while keeping a healthy core organism. Thus, nature finds a natural equilibrium between continuity and change, perfectly adapted for the surrounding environment, whether it alters significantly or not. Moreover, the concept of evolution involves the whole being, fully immersed in the process. It finds an echo in the metaphor of the ecosystem that has been used increasingly in the 2010s and 2020s to describe digital, platform-based networks of companies. An ecosystem metaphor applies equally elsewhere to describe many complex businesses.

I identified strongly with the concept because it elegantly describes the approach that we fashioned at LEGO. In previous chapters I have described many of the operational dysfunctions; these were overlaid on some strategic missteps. In the time shortly before I joined the company, a phase lasting from around 1995–2003, there was a period of undisciplined innovation: dozens of radically new products, departure from the concept of building with brick, disconnection from the most loyal consumers. It was a period of innovation and change that almost destroyed the business.

Strategy is a Process of Discovery

Repairing the company required a better strategy and one developed in partnership with operations and customer-facing employees and managers, as well as improved discipline and quality on operations.

There are three distinguishing features of a healthy evolutionary model to business strategy:

1. Readiness for change is *continual* and empirical – the organism should be constantly assessing, probing and experimenting, to discover whether different approaches will be more effective. Maintaining this demands continual discipline.
2. Actual change is *selective* and optimal – processes that are working fine and still appropriate are nurtured rather than altered.
3. The process is *holistic* – the entire organism should be immersed and involved in the evolutionary dynamic, at all times.

Leadership should practise continual experimentation and iteration, like the sciences, in Dr Goddard's view. He adds: '[French aviator and writer] Antoine de Saint-Exupéry said: "What separates us is not our aims – they all come to the same thing – but methods, the fruit of our reasoning." Strategies are all the same. Like values; you don't need to debate that kindness is better than cruelty. Those are givens. But how to be kind – the detail in the how is what separates success from failure. Strategies in business will be alike: strategies were always perfect. No one says that they want to destroy shareholder value, demotivate employees and irritate customers. The detail is the how: in leading a good life. How is always the difficulty.'

Leadership is necessary and it has to be of a style that engages the whole organism. There does have to be a single strategy, but adapted to reality as circumstances change. Execution of strategy is not just an unthinking roll-out as a one-off exercise, but a continual discipline of probing, experimenting and assessing, a process that is shaped by practical wisdom as well as theory. The board and the chief executive will take the lead, but all parts of the business are engaged in conversations and are open to adapting as they learn. As Dr Goddard adds: 'Execution comes before strategy. We discover what works by acting . . . Strategy is the roof, not the foundation.'

Developing and implementing strategy is more about asking questions than setting targets, a process of enquiry rather than prediction. In answering those questions experimentally, gradually our strategies will evolve.

We humans are a narrative species. Many of us in business management like to think we're only guided by the evidence and the data, but in practice much of our thinking is in stories. This means we must continually test and check our understanding against reality. In the unpredictable reality of governing or managing a real business, the strategic and operational issues are rarely neatly segregated; they come bundled up, like a gigantic knotted ball of ropes. This was certainly the case when LEGO hit crisis during my executive career, when the operational, design, marketing and strategic functions were in a state of dysfunction, with multiple problems compounding each other and certain individuals or functions becoming scapegoated. The company needed a better strategy, but that would not have resolved the problems on its own; and development of a smarter strategy without addressing the other issues would probably have led simply to a more prolonged death spiral. There is a fuller discussion of these problems, and how they were resolved, in the case study at the end of this chapter (*see also* pages 98–111).

In the 2020s, with the further rise of the digital economy, there is probably even greater need for a short line of communication between strategists and operational executives, and for strategy to be continually adapted, tested and refined with the help of continual dialogue, externally and internally. The CEOs of start-up companies whom I advise are in a state of almost continual flux as markets are prone not only to changing, but to becoming redefined. But, as I often have to remind them, this does not mean that everything has to change operationally, or that every new idea is automatically better than an older one.

The 'everyone-must-have-a-strategy' myth

Potentially even more disruptive than the concept of strategy as a rigid template or blueprint is an 'anything goes', unplanned state of affairs, where individual departments set their own strategy. An organisation in which there is too much inter-departmental rivalry may be prone to this. At LEGO in the early 2000s, the company lacked a unifying, coherent vision and strategy, as a result of the rather unplanned diversification. Each department would have its own strategy. When I questioned this, I would be challenged with a comment on the lines of: 'But I'm a vice-president, responsible for a department. Are you saying that I shouldn't have a strategy?' My reply would be: 'Yes.' Even as late as 2005–06, well into the turnaround, every department had its own strategy – and if you looked at them all, they were conflicting. For example, the head of distribution developed an online strategy – but without involving the IT function or the sales function. It had some coherence and merit as a plan, but it didn't involve the key partners and ended up getting dropped.

LEGO CEO Jørgen Vig Knudstorp, quite early in the turnaround phase, was pushing me for a strategy for the supply chain but I resisted, saying that supply needed to be fixed operationally first. I needed to better understand where the issues and challenges lay. Through the conversations that followed, Jørgen could see the sense in what I was saying, in part because his McKinsey training encourages detailed knowledge and data of the real business. He deserves enormous credit for staying open-minded and listening to my heretical views – it led to a very rich and deep discussion.

The learning point here is – and this links to the theme of Chapter 3, that the enterprise needs to be understood as an integrated, functioning organism – each constituent part needs to serve the central strategy, execute its responsibilities accordingly and coordinate with the others.

Dispelling these two myths can be liberating for a business. At LEGO, the process took some years for the beliefs fully to lose their power; moreover, there were complications because some of the innovations in the period 1995–2003 had much merit, such as the LEGO stores and theme parks. When things are going well in a business, not everything is perfect; by the same token, during a crisis there may be some promising developments that need nurturing rather than scrapping.

It would probably be widely accepted among managers and in business schools that operationalising each function improves efficiency. What we showed at LEGO is that it can improve innovation, creativity and development of strategy as well. Operations informed strategy, and vice versa. It was a symbiosis. Starting with the supply chain, we operationalised every function, ensuring we were dealing with reality. Understanding that operations need to be engaged in strategic development, rather than each operational function setting its own strategy, is a subtle and nuanced point.

Smarter strategy at LEGO

September 2005 was perhaps the most momentous, high-risk, pivotal moment of my career – and probably also of the life of the world's most-loved toy firm. Just over a year earlier LEGO had registered losses for 2003 that shocked everyone in the company and many observers and fans around the world too. Sales had plummeted by 26 per cent and the losses reached DKK935m (circa $150m) on turnover of DKK 6.8 billion (circa $1bn). There was an announcement on the web and results were shared worldwide. The Kristiansen family had financed the pay-run in 2004 so the run-up to the Christmas trading period 2005 was crucial. The phrase 'make-or-break' is probably over-used, but it perfectly and completely describes the stakes for LEGO in the closing weeks of 2005. A return to profit as part of a coherent strategy would rescue the company. Another year of heavy losses and it was doomed.

Many of us in the business were aware that the owning family, the Kristiansens, had been addressing this need for a central, guiding strategy. Major changes were expected and began to be unveiled in the period 2004–05. The third-generation family member Kjeld Kirk Kristiansen had been chief executive since 1994. He had appointed a five-member management team in the mid-1990s, whose primary objective had been growth with a view to leveraging the high recognition of the LEGO brand. This had been the start of diversification and expansion of products, with several successes but also burgeoning complexity and departure from the LEGO experience of creative play in some of the products.

Obviously, big changes were needed, if the company was to survive and remain independent. One of the biggest decisions took many by surprise. Key to understanding the decisions of the Kristiansen family is a deeper appreciation of how long-lasting business-owning families think and operate. They take a long-term view; they want a viable company or cluster of businesses to pass on to the next generation or, alternatively, a reinvention and set of new companies.[8] What it needed to do in the crucial period of strategic renewal in 2003–05 was return to the central promise of construction and play. At the stage of maximum peril, in 2003–04, the family could have sold to a major corporation. Some advisers informed them that the brand was worth more than the company – and advised the family that the logical thing to do was to sell.

The other thing to remember about long-lasting dynasties is that they have deep pockets and they practise counter-cyclical investing. They save during the boom years, so that in times of recession they can both continue their existing operations and invest in cut-priced assets. In the case of LEGO, the strategic ownership decisions are taken by KIRKBI, which is the Kirk Kristiansen family's private holding and investment company. Its purpose is to 'build a sustainable future for the family ownership through the generations'. True to this long-term vision, the family has invested heavily in environmental sustainability in recent years, for example.

The Kristiansens' sense of purpose comes from enhancing play and education for children, something that is not quantifiable, and which is a humanitarian vision about which Kjeld Kristiansen is particularly passionate. But while profit maximisation was not the priority, the company did have to return to profit, so the question became: how to save it and turn it around.

Their response to the record financial losses in the mid-2000s was to invest. This would only achieve the turnaround with significant changes to direction and personnel at the most senior executive levels of the company. Central to this was a key appointment: who would be the chief executive to head this crucial phase of the company's development?

Appointment of Jørgen Vig Knudstorp

For the first time in its history, the Kristiansen family decided in 2004 that they would appoint a non-family CEO. Kjeld stood down as chief executive, to take a full-time ownership role. His business brain and strategic assessment was first-rate; he decided that his strengths would be best deployed at board level, while recruiting a new chief executive to head the day-to-day operations.

Jørgen Vig Knudstorp was only 35 when he was appointed in 2004, internally promoted having impressed in his role as director of strategic development. A local individual, coming from near Billund, he had a PhD in business economics and had worked as a consultant for McKinsey. He had joined LEGO in 2001 in a strategic role. His CV was intellectually impressive, but did he have enough experience?

The risk with appointing a relatively inexperienced chief executive with an academic and consulting background is that they could engage in what I would call a superficial turnaround strategy: cutting costs and identifying a coherent strategy, but not sufficiently improving operations or harnessing the engagement of the whole enterprise. What I was to learn was that Jørgen would go far beyond the minimum necessary – indeed, that he was, and is, an exceptional individual, capable of thinking deeply as well as analytically, of understanding people and culture as well as strategy and operations. He is rare in combining high IQ and high EQ.

It did take a while for the wider company to accept that a non-family CEO was the 'real' chief executive. Jørgen's authority did come under challenge in the early months of his tenure – with a tacit belief that the 'real' authority lay with a family member. Additionally, of course, for many people it was difficult to accept senior decision-making from someone who was only 35. I heard comments such as: 'I don't agree with this. I want to talk to Kjeld.' Fortunately, Jørgen had an excellent relationship with Kjeld, who supported the new CEO. Any undermining of Jørgen's authority during those early months could have been fatal for the appointment and the turnaround. And although the appointment looked like a surprise from the outside, Jørgen had already been taking a lead role in the restructure in his previous post. Kjeld wanted him to continue in the same direction, with greater authority, so the promotion had an element of continuity.

Kjeld was not retiring, he was moving to an ownership role. This is distinct from executive management, but of fundamental importance. He and Jørgen developed the strategy for recovery and renewal together, and this was a formidable leadership team. Upon his appointment, Jørgen told the board bluntly that the business was not viable with its existing strategy and operations; that selling was an option if the owners did not want to turn the business around themselves and that turning it around was a long-term investment – it would not occur over a few quarters. Years later, he would recall how the banks were breathing down his neck during this period, asking for repayment of debt, and how the chief finance officer (CFO) bluntly told him that there was no identifiable profitable core. Hence cash management was a priority – indeed, an emergency.

The strategy that Kjeld and Jørgen developed consisted of three phases and was clearly articulated. There would be a two-year emergency programme called Manage for Cash, then a two-year phase, Manage for Value, then from 2008–09 onwards the objective would be Manage for Growth. Many budgets were at national or regional level, rather than broken down by product – so there was insufficient transparency about which products were profitable. The LEGOLAND theme parks, for example, were popular, yet loss-making. Key to the turnaround was the appointment of the chief finance officer. He was perfect for the role, being specialist in turnaround situations, exacting and forensic in understanding costs and where the value lies. He instilled the right systems. With the new team in charge, and a coherent phased strategy, I had increasing confidence that LEGO had a future.

At a strategic level, Jørgen's key insight was to focus on the core of the brand's value: what did LEGO mean, in the popular understanding? It meant creativity and play. So, he made decisions primarily on the products that fulfilled this promise and sold or closed others that had taken the company too far away.

Jørgen quickly realised that our reforms in the supply chain of transparency, performance and 'deliver what we promise' were central to becoming profitable; also that our insights could usefully inform designers and boost innovation. He forged partnerships between all key functions. Brand stretch and poor innovation in 1995–2003 had contributed to crisis; there was a need for a blend of core values and smarter innovation.

In a publicly listed company, there is pressure to make the quarterly growth targets which can encourage unrealistic ambitions and high pressure. The hazards in a private, family-owned firm like LEGO can be quite different: there is more concentrated ownership, which is an asset when the owners have made some big calls correctly, but it can mean that skewed priorities can persist. In the period 1990s–2003 the lead from the top, from the board, was based on a judgement that the brand was bigger than the business, leading them, quite understandably, to seek to leverage its value. A statement of strategic intent from the company in the mid-1990s ran: 'LEGO is not a toy – we want to be the strongest brand to families with children by 2005'. With hindsight, it can be seen that this led to too much experimentation in products that were not creative play with bricks, which was the common understanding of the LEGO experience so the brand was becoming diluted and many core fans felt let down. Some reining in of the diversification had begun around the turn of the millennium, with the ending of lines such as wristwatches and publishing in 2000, but there remained a proliferation of non-construction toys and a huge array of components.

It helped that Jørgen was alive to the issue; he in turn had been influenced by the analysis of Chris Zook, a consultant at Bain and co-author (with James Allen) of *Profit from the Core: A Return to Growth in Turbulent Times.* Zook had concluded that a company should focus on core products for a clearly defined and understood market. Any foray into an adjacent market should be selective and carefully planned and executed. A quote from Jørgen encapsulates this: 'One of the rules I stick to is you can really only build an adjacency to your core business every three to five years because it's such a major undertaking in terms of culture and capabilities. Rather than doing one adjacency every three to five years, we did three to five adjacencies every year so I think that's what nearly killed us.'[9]

It was impossible to deliver what we promised, if we had insufficient expertise in the delivery or understanding of what was being promised. The company lost focus and discipline. Of course in pharmaceuticals, where I spent the early years of my career, there is an inevitable discipline created by the fact that it is a heavily regulated sector, with products having to pass rigorous clinical trials. You can't just put an experimental drug out onto the market in the way that LEGO could try out a new design for a mini figure. Being in a lightly regulated sector can result in insufficient discipline, which brings with it a whole set of problems.

News of the record losses in 2003 caused shock externally. From the outside, to readers of the business pages, LEGO had been a success story for a couple of decades. The bricks were universally popular, there were high-profile licensing deals with the *Star Wars* and *Harry Potter* franchises, with LEGO developing mini figures based on characters in the movies and imaginative toys linked to these globally popular movies. But one of the hidden problems was that having major product lines closely tied to movie franchises meant that in a year like 2003, when there was neither a *Harry Potter* nor a *Star Wars* release, sales would slump. The deals had brought huge fluctuations in demand, compared with previous decades when there was a more gradual rise and fall in demand, anchored around the Christmas season. A more established brand, LEGO City, suffered from lack of investment and marketing spend. As discussed in Chapter 1 (*see also* page 18), we discovered that low sales had been a self-fulfilling prophesy.

There were unpopular products. The Jack Stone figure, larger than the standard LEGO mini figures, was designed as an All-American action hero, with a suite of toys centred around him, mostly aircraft and motor vehicles, many from the emergency services – but it never really caught the imagination of children. Jack Stone was launched in 2001 but dropped just two years later. Galidor comprised a set of bespoke figurines that were linked to a short-lived children's sci-fi TV series of the same name. Clickets was the brand name for toys aimed at girls, including bracelets. The triangular packaging had a flaw in the design, in that it featured a flap that would be stuck down, but which in practice was prone to small tears that impaired the image. After being made aware of the problem, the response was to increase the marketing spend.

While an innovative company will accept that not all new products will be popular and highly profitable – indeed, if there are zero failures you are almost certainly not being innovative enough – failure of some new ideas should not lead to crisis. Creative innovation should involve experimentation and piloting, and being prepared to acknowledge when something hasn't worked and learn from it. What matters is that collectively you are adaptable and you haven't bet the house on a risky innovation. During this period, designers and strategists did not appear to be talking enough to the fans, including the adult fans, and there were innovations that departed from the central building brick, which is what most people understand as the 'LEGO' experience. The cull of products was selective; Jørgen looked at the system as a whole, as well as individual lines. Some toys that were loss-making at that time were retained, because they were recoverable and central to the identity. For example, the preschool toys were retained as a means of introducing children to the LEGO experience at an early age. An unsuccessful rebrand was reversed, with the DUPLO brand, which had first been used in 1968, reintroduced.

The firm had created LEGOLAND theme parks – they were popular, but also loss-making. LEGO was a manufacturing company, not specialist in visitor attractions. In aggregate, setting up several disparate initiatives, each requiring different specialisms, tends to increase complexity at the centre in an exponential, not linear fashion. Individually, some of the innovations may make sense, but there has to be an understanding at the centre of the implications of managing all of them, simultaneously.

When Kjeld Kristiansen approved the sale of the theme parks, this sent a powerful signal. It made sense to transfer them to a more specialist management. LEGOLAND, however, was Kjeld's baby. If his business sense overruled any emotional attachment, this was a powerful signal that the family were serious about rescuing the company.

Faulty narratives, untested hypotheses

As a mitigating factor for some of the innovative flops and strategic weaknesses at LEGO, there had been significant technological and demographic changes altering the toy market in the 1990s and early 2000s. LEGO had to adapt and some of its innovations were successful. Electronic games were increasing rapidly in sophistication, play times for many children had become shorter. Birth rates in LEGO core markets in Western Europe and North America had fallen, household spending on toys fell consequently and profit margins were being squeezed. Meanwhile, many smaller toy shops were closing, with the industry becoming dominated by retail giants. In the US the huge outlets of relevance were Toys R Us, Walmart and Target following this consolidation; meanwhile, online sales, especially through Amazon, were growing rapidly from the 2000s onwards.[10] This trend accentuated with the further rise of the digital giants, a boost to online ordering during the Covid-19 pandemic in 2020–21, with many bricks-and-mortar stores closing in what became known as the 'retail apocalypse'.

On the other hand, the number of middle-class households was rising around the world during the 1990s and early 2000s, and there were many opportunities for the enterprising toy company. When change is rapid and complex, it is essential to be wary of simpler narratives taking hold and becoming adopted as a complete explanation for developing trends, which in addition to being complex are prone to unexpected twists. It is particularly important not to make simplistic, linear extrapolations. When new technology emerges and products using it start to gain popularity, there will be at least some replacement of an old technology, but this does not necessarily mean that the latter becomes obsolete (although in some cases it does – it's complicated). Examples of traditional products which dipped in popularity, or fell precipitously, only to stage an unlikely comeback include vinyl records and jigsaw puzzles.[11] Another example was construction-style toys, including LEGO, which proved to be exceptionally popular during the lockdown measures instigated in response to the Covid pandemic in the early 2020s. What is missing from electronic interaction is the sense of touch – one of the core senses and central to the human experience. When everything appears to be changing, some things stay the same.

Anticipating trends requires constant monitoring and being prepared for unexpected developments. A narrative that some held in the toy industry in the 1990s and early 2000s was based on a notion that the future was electronic only. The real picture that emerged during the turnaround, especially after Jørgen Vig Knudstorp took over, was different. Yes, electronics were changing the market, but it was not the only change and some customer preferences stayed constant. What was more significant still was that part of the problem for LEGO during this period came from moving too far away from the core brick-building experience. The most dedicated fans told us: 'You've lost your way.' The lesson was clear: to be genuinely a LEGO toy, construction and creativity had to be central to the experience. If electronics were to feature, they needed to be combined with the brick. Reducing complexity and the number of components also became key objectives.

Accelerating the progress towards the turnaround, in my experience, were two decisive factors: the fact that Jørgen Vig Knudstorp, the incoming CEO, totally grasped the importance of an evolving and sophisticated approach to strategy, working in partnership with operations; and the Visual Factory approach, anchored around weekly performance briefings which I introduced to the company, which transformed both accountability and performance. A detailed description of the Visual Factory approach will be the subject of Chapter 7 (*see also* pages 127–144).

Summary

The twin popular myths of strategy-formation – that it is either a rigid formula for success developed in secret by the C-suite prior to a roll-out, or by contrast an unplanned state of affairs in which everyone with a managerial role is free to pursue their own strategy – have prevented the adoption of a more mature approach. My own experience and observations are now supported by an increasing amount of business literature. I have referenced *Execution: The Discipline of Getting Things Done* by Ram Charan and Larry Bossidy and quoted Jules Goddard, author of *Uncommon Sense, Common Nonsense: Why some organisations consistently outperform others*, a more recent articulation of the enquiring, iterative approach to strategy development. But while operations should not be pursuing their own strategy, they should be involved as equal partners, informing and shaping strategic development as well as ensuring that the business as a whole organism delivers what it promises.

Key principles from this chapter

- Strategy is fetishised by many business students and graduates – yet ironically it is also misunderstood. There are two popular misconceptions: 1) That strategy is a rigid plan devised and rolled out by an elite; and 2) That each department has a strategy.
- Instead, strategy is better understood as iteration and adaptation through continual dialogue and enquiry. There does need to be a single strategy, but it is in continual evolution in response to markets, technology and other changes. Execution muscle must always be maintained and business leadership requires nurturing and maintenance, as well as agility and change.
- Strategy formation and adaptation needs to be *continual*, *selective* and *holistic*.
- At LEGO, unplanned innovation in line with a strategy of change in response to digital technology and change markets led the company to crisis. A key lesson was to be selective about investing in a new adjacency.

- Brand stretch can result from strategic failure. As an example, LEGO was not a brand that could be attached to any merchandise that may appeal to children. It *was* a toy, after all. Yet some innovations from the 1990s were successful. During a restructure or turnaround, a deep analysis is essential so you can hold on to products and services that are successful, or have potential.

- When everything appears to be changing, some things stay the same. Vinyl records, jigsaws and LEGO toys are examples of long-established products that have seen revival and growth in popularity in the early decades of the twenty-first century.

How to implement the principles

- Board discussions, and strategic conversations at the executive level, need to be anchored in reality. It is healthy to treat significant statements or conclusions about an aspect of the business as a hypothesis to be questioned and challenged rather than a definitive conclusion.

- Don't confuse the map for the territory: it is helpful to have a balance of qualitative and quantitative information to guide you on what is going on in the organisation, but no reports tell the full picture.

- Business leaders need to keep themselves informed with all the key stakeholders, including customers. They need to understand what the brand means to the consumer before deciding how to update their offerings, or assess whether certain products or services have a future. A traditional product may be more popular than an innovative one and brand stretch can be fatal.

- Functional heads throughout the business have a leadership role, but it involves learning how to support, inform and shape the central strategy, not set their own one.

Chapter 6
Ensure the Whole Business Collaborates

A prejudice that I have fought throughout my whole career is that manufacturing or the supply chain is seen as transactional, even 'dirty'. A common approach in business management is to divide the business into 'money-making' functions, distinct from support services that are treated as just a cost base. This is a false distinction. All parts contribute to creating value. Every function has costs and every function adds value – or at least, it ought to. A supply chain is a way of connecting people – it's not just a cost base. The whole business has to collaborate – this is a challenging discipline, not a cosy togetherness; it means confronting and not postponing difficult conversations and addressing the need for trade-offs. It means having the right people in the discussions, irrespective of their function or hierarchical status.

The smartest inventors and entrepreneurs get this. In an interview for this book, the technology entrepreneur Tony Fadell, inventor of the iPod and Nest Labs, observed: 'I was told [early on in my career] that the design team did everything – but my reaction is: What? No – how about engineering, operations? The way I look at it, you as an individual in any large company need to go beyond your silo; learn about other things, make sure you speak their language. You are more powerful if you want to move up – you need to know these different languages. Many people don't want to translate between them, but you're more powerful if you can. It's an imperative if people can understand what it takes, not just ideas, but who's doing the work? It doesn't just take a design team, every person is a designer – whether you're in operations, HR. You take the operations mentality: yes, process, shedding light in.

'I tell everyone: Don't just look down at your feet, what you're doing today; look more, look up and down, and look left and right, across the disciplines, look across, build those relationships, that knowledge, translational skills.'

The founders of the online retail behemoth Amazon, from its earliest days, had a similar understanding of the importance of execution, logistics, supply and all parts of the business being coordinated. In the early 2000s, most of the dotcom start-ups famously failed to survive more than a couple of years, burning through investors' cash while struggling to monetise their web traffic. Those that succeeded had strengths in traditional disciplines such as logistics and managerial execution. One of those was Amazon, which is a massive global tech firm at the time of writing, but which was just one of many young online retailers in the late 1990s and at the turn of the millennium. Among the disciplines of Amazon's founding teams was to concentrate on the customer's needs and to understand how to build a large, low-margin business. To this end, back in the 1990s they had met and interviewed executives from the supermarket chain Walmart to understand in depth how to do this – not an obvious path to take for Silicon Valley technology entrepreneurs.[12] From the earliest days of the company, its founders devoted many hours to understanding logistical business disciplines, matching demand and supply, and cost control, that probably came across as dull and unsexy to many rivals and their venture capitalist backers.

Core competence

The emphasis on the importance of delivery, supply and logistics, in addition to design, marketing and strategy, may be challenged by some managers and business students. How does this relate to the concept of core competence? Surely a business has to invest heavily in specialist functions that are key to gaining a competitive edge, while outsourcing commoditised processes – e.g. hiring DHL to do delivery, or ADP to run the payroll? There *should* be a hierarchy, the argument goes, because some skills are simultaneously more important and less common.

This objection is valid, but only up to a point. It is a nuanced argument. To take the example of Amazon, it is true that key to competitive advantage are features such as the range of products, competitive costing, ease of purchase online and ability to scale. But the delivery still has to be reliable and effective. All functions are part of a harmonised whole and it is smart management, in practice, to treat all functions as partners. In a heavily commoditised function, you are still dealing with people; partners who may have important insights from their intimate knowledge of their part of the value chain, which will always be superior, on those particular aspects, to the knowledge at the centre. Yes, there are certain specialisms that are more equal than others – for example, imaginative toy designers at LEGO, or software developers at a web company – but their efforts are worthless without a well-coordinated network of specialists to bring their ideas to the customer. Reserving use of the term 'value-adding' only for certain functions is an illusion and creates a dangerous divide. It is the whole enterprise that adds value (or not, as the case may be).

While it makes sense to outsource functions in which you do not have world-class expertise and where a specialist firm can do a better job, it is wisest to do so on the basis of capability and value for money, not on cost-cutting alone, or on a perception that certain functions are lower status. Moreover, you can never outsource responsibility and your partners are part of the wider ecosystem. In LEGO, the bias in favour of marketing and design and against manufacturing and supply, and its efforts to position itself as a branding specialist, led to the decision in the early 2000s to outsource factories. It did not work out as planned. As the operations executive responsible both at the time of the outsourcing, and when the process was reversed a few years later, my insights are hopefully valuable to anyone wishing to deepen their knowledge both of what constitutes 'core competence' and how the core must be connected to the rest.

Lesson from LEGO: Outsourcing – high stress, negotiations, and a U-turn

In 2005, LEGO returned to profit after a near-terminal crisis. However, in 2006, we emerged from one headache – the financial losses of 2003–04, to encounter another. There was one legacy of the historically junior status of operations that we had to confront. Among many senior figures there remained a prevailing view that LEGO had become a design, sales and marketing specialist and that manufacturing was not a core specialism. In the early 2000s, outsourcing manufacturing was hugely fashionable, especially by Western companies to the comparatively low-cost emerging manufacturing business clusters in East Asia, such as China and Vietnam. As discussed, there is logic in sticking to your core competence and outsourcing certain functions

to others with better expertise. Since the end of that decade there has been a growing evidence base showing that
outsourcing should be primarily on the basis of quality,[13]
rather than cost-savings and smart executives seek to establish partnerships on that basis.

My problem at LEGO during this period was not the
logic but the judgement: my view – and I was not alone
internally – was that we were world leaders in moulding
competence, which was and is of central importance to the
LEGO brick and the experience for the consumer. I had no
problem with outsourcing electronics components, distribution or the LEGOLAND theme parks – but moulding?
There had been issues to attend to, but they had been more
to do with packing and the supply chain than the quality of
moulding, which was world-class and unbeatable. Moreover, we were rapidly getting on top of the packing issues.

At the time I was too junior to have influenced the
outsourcing decision. Instead, I inherited it. There was
a celebratory air at a dinner attended to mark the deal,
secured with the leading global electronics and manufacturing specialist Flextronics. At this event, there were
only around five LEGO executives and around 30 lawyers
and consultants. This jarred. It felt a little like doing a lap
of honour with the trophy before the cup final had even
started. The real test of an outsourcing relationship is in
the delivery and we rapidly hit problems.

Ensure the Whole Business Collaborates

The changes involved moving a manufacturing operation from Switzerland to Hungary, and from Enfield, US, to Juárez, Mexico; handing over our Czech plant and closing a Korean site. Flextronics would run the Czech, Hungary and Mexico plants, while a small manufacturing operation was retained by LEGO at Billund. Our outsourcing partner, later rebranded as Flex, was and still is a highly professional outfit and, indeed, we learned much from them. The problems lay in how the relationship worked out, to do with contractual issues, misunderstanding their business model, unrealistic expectations and some bad luck. Some of the blame lay on our side: I recall expressing doubt over the service levels that we specified; we had never achieved those ourselves! From the supplier's side, Flextronics were optimistic about savings that could be achieved. The clash in business model exacerbated problems and led to recurring issues, which should really have been identified at the negotiating stage. For Flextronics, each factory was a profit centre, whereas a factory within the LEGO company does not have to meet profit targets as a unit – only the company as a whole does. So if, during the outsourcing relationship, we felt that Flextronics should absorb costs, or should invest in more frequent maintenance on moulds, for example, this request was in direct conflict with the way in which their business was structured and their managers incentivised. Over the course of the next couple of years, some 70–80 per cent of my time was spent in dealing with the outsourcing relationship and the frequent issues that arose. There was a certain irony: we had moved out of a crisis phase, yet my stress levels were as high as ever.

It had been heart-rending to oversee the closure of the Enfield manufacturing site. I was impressed and deeply moved by those long-serving LEGO staff patiently training their new Mexican colleagues, knowing that their own plant was closing and the economic future of themselves and their workmates was uncertain. One matter on which Jørgen Vig Knudstorp and the senior team were clear was that we were going to be honest with the staff. I myself had been on the receiving end of such a decision, when Glaxo shut the production lines in Dartford, England in the mid-1990s, including those where Paul Ferarrio, myself and others had achieved spectacular productivity improvements. The senior Glaxo leaders had kept too much information to themselves until late in the process, I felt. At LEGO, we made sure that the staff were the first to hear and arrangements were made to look after the welfare of the departing staff – for example, ensuring that healthcare costs were covered for ongoing treatment. I daresay we weren't perfect, but it was notable that, when a TV journalist interviewed some LEGO staff asking for their reactions to the plant closure, they expressed sadness but little anger, and even some praise for how managers had handled the process.

Ensure the Whole Business Collaborates

During the outsourcing experience, we did learn from Flextronics. Their documentation and processes were excellent. In order to prepare for the transfer, we had to document all of our equipment and processes thoroughly, which was an excellent discipline that we retained. They were also expert in scaling up and down with staffing levels, using temporary staff – another valuable lesson.

Overall, however, the arrangement was not working and we came to negotiate an exit. LEGO was a bigger brand, but a smaller business than Flextronics, and by 2008 we decided through discussion that there was a mutual interest in LEGO taking manufacturing back in-house. This meant regaining control for us, a relatively small loss of business for them and an end to the headaches for both of us. For me, there was a personal risk in taking a lead in negotiating the return to in-house production because I was known as a sceptic of outsourcing. There were whispers that I hadn't done enough to make it work. Jørgen quashed such talk, publicly stating that I had done my best to make the partnership effective. On the other hand, there were others who cheered when manufacturing 'came home'.

Looking back, the big error of judgement on our side in the outsourcing venture was to assume that manufacturing – especially moulding – was not a core expertise for LEGO. The experience confirmed to us that this was not the case. The engineering expertise within LEGO was world-class and there were tremendous advantages in being in-house, in terms of manufacturing innovation, adaptability and control. In the subsequent years of growth, our brilliant, pioneering engineers devised superb innovations and collectively were able to scale up quickly.

My reservations about outsourcing manufacturing were never ideological. The judgement should always be about pragmatic business sense. For specialist electronics, we outsourced successfully to a Chinese firm. For distribution, we consolidated to three major regional hubs – Europe, North America and China – run by specialist firms. The LEGO-LAND theme park was sensibly transferred to Merlin, a specialist at visitor attractions. All these were effective because the higher levels of expertise necessary were not available in-house. What cannot be outsourced, however, is accountability. In the case of the theme parks, these were customer-facing businesses, with our logo prominent. As far as the public were concerned, they were LEGO services. Any comment or complaint – be it around wheelchair accessibility, queues or food – would still come to us. We devolved day-to-day responsibility for operations to Merlin, but liaised very closely on customer service and customer feedback.

Summary

The importance of respecting the contribution of every function is closely linked to the subject of Chapter 3 –

understanding the business as a complex organism, with interconnected and changing parts (*see also* pages 47–71). It does not mean abandoning the concept of core competence. To take an analogy with an actual organism, the heart and lungs are more important than most other parts, but you still need the whole to function optimally.

Key principles from this chapter

- It is illogical and unhelpful to denote supply and operations as junior in status to strategy, design and branding. Everything has to be in partnership.
- Amazon founders and the iPhone inventor Tony Fadell emphasise the importance of strategists and designers knowing about engineering and operations. Much competitive advantage lies in execution.
- Core competence is a helpful concept in terms of helping managers to understand what is critical to competitive edge – unique or rare capabilities that are difficult to imitate or expensive to build and that make the brand distinctive and valuable – but these strengths will only add competitive edge if the whole enterprise is well-coordinated, with the contributions of all harnessed and appreciated.
- Outsourcing is best done on the basis of quality of service, not cost-cutting, and outsourced providers must be seen as partners. It is important to assess whether their business model clashes with yours.

- You cannot outsource responsibility.

How to implement the principles

- Be prepared to operationalise and strategise together – it's common that operational and strategic problems are interlinked. These initiatives were in parallel during the turnaround at LEGO, not sequential, because the factors were closely linked and supply was in need of remedial action with some changes that could not await implementation of a new strategy.
- When seeking to assess core competence, engage in rigorous analysis; don't rely on hunches or an assumption that manufacturing or supply is automatically commoditised or of lower value than branding, marketing or design.
- Factors to measure or otherwise assess in gauging core competence include uniqueness of the company's offering, level and scarcity of skills in a potential core competence and whether the in-house capability is world-class.

Chapter 7
The Visual Factory

It was not the most conventional family outing on a Sunday. I took my wife Sati and our daughter to a windowless room inside a building on the LEGO factory site in Enfield, Connecticut, and we papered some walls in white. We drew columns and rows on the walls, ready for critical business information to be entered, to help the supply team and other functions ensure that the toy factories were producing the right goods, to the right quality, at the right time, and supplying the stores. This was to be the control room, I explained, for what I would call the Visual Factory: for getting operations right and fixing the North American LEGO operations. Our daughter didn't get to play with any LEGO toys that day, but she knew she was helping other children receive their preferred toys in tip-top condition – ultimately more satisfying for a child, don't you think?

Don't judge me too harshly. We had fun papering – even if it was only in the one colour. Afterwards, we went out for a family meal (and Sati and I are still married, 20 years on). The family stood to benefit, if I could ensure that this idea helped safeguard the viability of my employer, LEGO, in turn helping my family's financial security.

One of the origins for my idea was rooted in my experience early on in my career, as a young operator and manager, sitting in wasteful and unproductive meetings. As we left, I would overhear colleagues mutter: 'Well, that was a waste of time,' – typically said by individuals who never pushed for a change in the way of doing things! Meetings that revolve around presentations can be stale and directionless, sucking energy out of the team. I perceived a difference between myself and some of my colleagues. For me, a meeting had to have a purpose – to drive performance forward. For others, for those who enjoyed giving a presentation, the meeting *was* the purpose.

The Visual Factory, however, is much more than a style of meeting: it is a way of doing business. It is centred around a weekly operation briefing, which provides a concise yet full overview, a perfect induction to a company's operations, a reliable antidote to complacency yet also a platform on which to receive deserved recognition. It is, in short, the company at its best, in one small room for 30 or 40 minutes on a Friday morning.

One of its most valuable roles, especially for readers of a book like this, is that it is a direct way of putting into practice the progressive yet often abstract-sounding concepts that we in the profession of management yearn continually for – agility, transparency, efficiency, effectiveness, innovation, teamwork. If we've read an inspiring book or heard a talk by a charismatic speaker and are filled with enthusiasm to transform culture and performance, there is sometimes a gap, if perhaps only a small one, between the concept and the practice. We begin the next working day full of ideas, but we are not always sure of the first step. So how will we actually do things differently?

Try this, dear reader, try this. It is a weekly performance briefing and it can be highly effective, even transformative. The first rule of Visual Factory is: you stick to the principles, you don't let things slide. And the principles are straightforward:

- Membership – you have the right people in the room (which may be virtual, of course) – not based on hierarchy.
- Timekeeping – you start and end on time.
- Culture of collaboration – all functions have equal status.
- You stick to the 'Vital Few' points of data. No waffle, no printouts!
- Accountability – you speak to your action, you ensure fairness.
- Overview of the whole value chain.

In more detail:

Membership – having the right people in the room. In conventional meetings, in my experience, sometimes the wrong people are in the room – they aren't directly involved in the tasks being discussed, or the right people are absent – because they are in a different department or 'silo', or considered too junior. The idea of the Visual Factory is to encourage teamwork across departmental lines, to have everyone involved who needs to be, and no one who doesn't, to support collaboration and effectiveness. Individuals taking part range from those directly involved in operations to senior vice-presidents, with everyone encouraged to contribute. There is a culture of being 'forced to cooperate'. It also sets a great stage for everyone to learn about each other's areas.

Timekeeping – the meetings are every week, early in the morning on a Friday, and should be limited to half an hour – or 40 minutes in exceptional circumstances. They start on time. To begin with, I instilled this discipline by not recapping the start of the meeting to late entrants; later, I became stricter still and locked the door at the start. On one occasion, a dozen people arrived ten minutes late for a meeting and made light of the matter when I challenged them. Here, my grounding in operating costs from Wellcome came into play. I said: 'You have just wasted 120 minutes of company resources.' In the Visual

Factory there are no screens, no speeches, no reports – just actions.

Culture – at LEGO, by working across silos, we sought to end the idea of operations as 'dirty' or junior. There is an emphasis on honest dialogue. Style of conversation lies at the core of setting a culture: how we talk to each other sets the tone on how the business is run. There is an emphasis on being candid and reality-based, able to raise and openly discuss tough questions and find solutions, avoiding being stilted, political or back-covering with a tendency to blame or scapegoat. Attendees are from different specialisms and levels; from vice-presidents to relatively junior operational staff, and in meetings there is a sense of equal status, with everyone encouraged to contribute and ask questions.

Data and information – it is a continual challenge to have enough of the right information in a business – a focus on the key metrics. We instilled the concept of the 'Vital Few'. White Board meetings (*see also* pages 134–5) help encourage a focus on sticking to the essential data – that which helps the business in strategy and operations. Being multi-disciplinary is essential: for example, it is not necessarily helpful to know that production and efficiency are maximised, if it is for a product for which there is insufficient demand, so production, packing, sales and marketing all have to be engaged.

Accountability – while we work in teams, each person has to be accountable individually. The White Board system allocates a task to a named individual. It is colour coded: Green for 'In control', Red for 'Discussion required', and Blue or Black for 'Information'. In practice, everyone assigned an action will be working with others to accomplish it, but it is essential to have a clear line of responsibility. Both good and poor performance is transparent. This rests on the concept of the 'shadow of the future' – an elegant phrase coined by the thinker Robert Axelrod to describe the continual expectation of mutual responsibilities and the benefits of cooperation; everyone knows that what we commit to do one week will be subject to a check the following week. Dispensing with meeting minutes also helps: the psychological effect of picking up a pen and writing on a board, knowing that you would have to talk to it and that, if necessary, it will be followed up the following week, is powerful. We think and learn as we write, so you are more engaged than when passively listening and watching presentations in a conventional meeting. Fairness is a key aspect of accountability: it is necessary to hold people to account, but not in an oppressive way. It is equally important to prevent scapegoating of individuals wrongly blamed for a missed goal or system failure.

Understanding the whole value chain – a key concept is that one should be able to walk into the Visual Factory at any time and gain a clear understanding of the business within ten minutes, based on the information on the board. The Visual Factory is an excellent way of introducing new staff to the business as they can grasp key elements of operations and performance in a way that is quicker and more accurate than reading long presentations or meeting minutes. All functions within the business are seen as equal, mutually dependent parts; none is seen as being 'superior' to the others. Also, HR and pay policy has to support this cooperation; in my early years at LEGO, I came across perverse incentives in the bonus system – for example, a bonus to reach 10,000 bricks per hour, irrespective of whether the right components were being produced. The focus should always be on the customer (retailer) *and* the consumer. One of the challenges in my early years at LEGO was instilling a greater respect for retailers. There was rapid change and consolidation in the retail sector during my early years in LEGO and there has been further change since. We began the practice of operations executives attending sales meetings to get to know retail customers. This was considered unusual, but it strengthened our approach as it meant that there was a deeper understanding of customer needs running through the organisation. It helped ensure that we delivered what we promised – and that what we promised was what the retailers and the consumers wanted.

Context of setting up the Visual Factory

This is how it came about at LEGO. And this is how the supply chain assumed a leadership role. In 2004, we needed a new planning system. It occurred to me that there was much I could learn from my past experience. In the late 1990s at Glaxo, there had been a major implementation of a systemic information system known as BPICS. I had been too junior at the time to be directly overseeing its implementation; what I recalled was that it had initially gone disastrously wrong – inventory went missing, contributing to a financial loss – but in time the problems were resolved. If we could learn from the Glaxo veterans, on what to do and what not to do, what can go wrong and why accurate and relevant data is so important, this could save much time and wasted resources. It seemed an ideal opportunity.

So, I asked some of the Glaxo managers if they would give a presentation to us and they agreed. I took around 15 LEGO colleagues with me to Ware in Hertfordshire, England, for a one-day conference. As is often the way, an unexpected by-product of the meeting turned out to be the most valuable outcome. They mentioned a form of meeting known as the 'White Board' meeting. This involved dispensing with minutes, PowerPoint presentations, even chairs or a table. Instead, it would involve a focused discussion for around half an hour in front of a white board with actions – and names attached to each action – written up in prominent, colour-coded text on the board, to be erased once completed. The description of this style of meeting took probably no more than ten minutes out of an eight-hour set of presentations, but it struck me immediately as an approach with much potential. Ideas that had been forming in my mind for years, from first hearing expressions of frustration over wasteful meeting habits early on in my career to beginning to sharpen the sense of accountability in my early months in LEGO, coalesced.

This, I decided, would be key to our way of management for the turnaround. It appealed to me in every sense: no waste, no waffle, a focus on the essentials and clear accountability. By contrast, a conventional meeting in which people are sat at desks, looking at a presentation and often glancing down at their phones, and which often runs on too long, lacks energy and focus, and wastes time that is better spent completing the agreed actions. How many of us have been here? We had already begun to exercise greater accountability and a weekly meeting. From that moment on, they were to be held on the 'White Board' principles, in the Visual Factory.

A minor factor behind the decision to set up the Visual Factories was that as a senior manager, I was travelling regularly between Denmark and the US, and had near-permanent jet lag – keeping the meetings short while people were standing up helped me stay awake! Changing the approach to how we held weekly meetings might sound like a modest initiative, but it had a transformational effect on business culture and ultimately performance. There were several key features that ensured that the Visual Factory had a lasting and positive impact. These were:

- Every six months, the Visual Factory was reset – that is, the data and subjects of discussion were reviewed and some data was pruned. The reset was done by appointing a team of four or five people, from different functions, to remove irrelevant issues and data from the boards. Data is a means to an end. The purpose of highlighting certain indicators was to improve service to the customer, not information for its own sake or to celebrate past successes. We sought to be disciplined in this, keeping the focus on what really mattered. The Visual Factory worked best when the key indicators were kept to a minimum and the practice of pinning up printouts of spreadsheets on the wall discouraged. For example, the fill rate – the proportion of customer orders that the company can meet – is a key indicator. It needs to be above 70–80 per cent. The point was relevance, not comprehensiveness, in the data presented and discussed. This meant being selective.
- Within a year or so, the Visual Factory approach was adopted by manufacturing in Billund and thereafter spread slowly throughout the company, and in due course, to other

businesses too. I felt proud in later years, when visiting a site, that the local managers would invite me to a meeting to demonstrate how they had adopted this approach. As a result of the Visual Factory, we began making better, faster decisions and, because there was more transparency about performance, there was rapid awareness of how much better we were doing, which, in turn, led to greater collective confidence, further boosting performance, in a virtuous circle.

How it works in theory

We established that the Visual Factory worked in practice. Later, I discovered that it also works in theory; strikingly similar principles have emerged from academic research. Yves Morieux, head of organisational development at the Boston Consulting Group, is the author of *Six Simple Rules: How to Manage Complexity Without Getting Complicated* (with co-author Peter Tollman, Harvard Business Press, 2014), based on findings from game theory and organisational sociology. Independently, he developed an approach to organisational management with the same core principles that we had introduced in the LEGO supply chain, with the help of the Visual Factory. The rules are:

- Understand what your people do – engage in reality, not the proxy of reports or reporting lines.

- Reinforce integrators – these are existing managers whom you reinforce so that they have power and interest to make others cooperate. You do this by removing layers. When there are too many layers, people are too far from the action. Key Performance Indicators (KPIs) and metrics are poor proxies for reality.

- Increase total quantity of power – empower everyone to use their judgement, their intelligence. Encourage them to take the risk to cooperate.

- Extend the shadow of the future – expose people to the effects of their actions or inactions.

- Increase reciprocity – create incentives to work together as necessary for operations. When there is limited reciprocity, you generate the problem of 'dysfunctional self-sufficiency'.

- Reward those who cooperate. Don't blame failure, but rather failure to ask for help.

Yves Morieux has recorded how the arbitrary delineation between 'hard' and 'soft' managerial tasks, respectively focusing on processes and relationships, creates complicatedness, frustration, inefficiency and problems with quality. So-called 'hard' approaches result in a complicated array of metrics, KPIs, incentives and committees, while 'soft' approaches often focus on relationships in a way that is segregated from tasks, or ignores areas where difficult trade-offs need to be negotiated (the problems that arise from the arbitrary distinction between 'hard' and 'soft' managerial issues form the subject of Chapter 12, *see also* pages 193–201).

Around 2008, a few years after we established the Visual Factory, Yves observed us in practice and recognised the strong similarities with the approach he had developed. He summarised these in an interview for this book. The Visual Factory is not a meeting, he observed, it is more akin to a performance. More than the mere exchange of communication, it is where the real organisation comes together to make the essential negotiations and agreements that will deliver the necessary products and services. It deals with reality, not proxies. He adds: 'In the Visual Factory you don't discuss structures, processes, systems, the formal organisation. You discuss the real organisation, the real issues. For me, it is a cognitive device to understand real issues . . . The second characteristic is [that] it is a problem-solving artefact.

'The Visual Factory is simple: there is no laptop, no printout, issues are written on the wall. And names of the people accountable for finding solutions and milestones with estimated and agreed-upon deadlines for the right solutions. People agree on the deadlines. Second, the people in the room are those directly involved in the issues. They are not their boss or reports, they are the people who know about the issues and who are part of the issues as opposed to delegating up or down to other people with a less accurate understanding of the issues.'

It could be said that individuals are exposed or cornered in the Visual Factory, which makes it sound threatening. The way in which it is introduced has to be balanced, so that people have coaching and support in addition to being challenged. The real purpose, Yves Morieux observed, is not so much that people are cornered, but that the truth is: you are confronted with reality. This may be uncomfortable for those who have not delivered on their actions – but the stress and difficulties are far greater when the truth is ignored and problems are allowed to fester and worsen. In practice at LEGO, people saw it as liberating because it was a way to voice their real concerns and see progress in action, on a weekly basis.

Yet although the practices of the Visual Factory, or Morieux's six rules, are well established intellectually and in practice, they remain a minority practice; the bureaucracy, frustration and sub-optimal performance of the 'hard and soft' approach to management remain commonplace.

Wider influence

I know the practice has spread to other workplaces, though inevitably with local variations. Niels Duedahl, CEO of the Danish energy and telecoms group Norlys at the time of writing this book, is a former colleague of mine at LEGO.

As discussed earlier in Chapter 3 (*see also* page 52), he was influenced by my insistence that senior executives should have a good knowledge of operational detail and not sit too far above the organisational reality. Niels uses the Visual Factory as the basis for the way in which the whole enterprise at Norlys is organised and run. In an interview for this book, he observes: 'My company is run 100 per cent in the Bali Padda style. I have Visual Factory every Friday. I really believe in that concept. It kills excuses – people stop talking about IT systems not working and start taking responsibility. I use Visual Factory even to brief the board. It's the culture, it's how we address [it]. [There is a] link to the company's values. It's totally [transparent] – if you're not in there performing. That's your legacy, Bali. [It's been the] key driver for success in 11 years [at Norlys]. [A more] sophisticated [version] has driven us to a higher level. How do you sustain resilience? Discipline – continuing until it works.'

The Preface to this book (*see also* pages 1–6) contains a typical interaction at a Visual Factory briefing, where a big decision was made, with the reasons given, clearly and openly in front of the staff. While the direct accountability could be seen as almost brutal, important principles are fairness and clarity; it should never become intimidating. Yes, there is a laser-like focus on accountability and performance, but this is geared towards helping ensure you deliver what you promise. The approach can and should be accompanied by the practices of acknowledging people's performance and contribution, and ensuring psychological safety. Clarity of accountability helps prevent individuals from failing in their responsibilities, but also helps prevent scapegoating – individuals being wrongly blamed for someone else's mistakes, or for a technological fault beyond their control. In this way, to borrow Niels' phrase, it 'kills excuses', helps ensure we are always dealing with reality and that those who have achieved are recognised.

Summary

The Visual Factory approach is anchored around the weekly performance briefing, but it constitutes a way of doing business geared to effective execution, it is not just a meeting format. Maintaining discipline to ensure its effectiveness requires constant effort. The three curses of organisational management – waste, waffle and ego – seem to creep into the most efficient of practices over time, even in well-run businesses with highly educated executives. At times within LEGO, I would visit a briefing and see printouts of data – too long and detailed for anyone to have time to read – pinned up on the wall. I would go round the room and take them down.

Key to understanding the role of the Visual Factory is to see it as an operational briefing and central to operations. Far more than a form of communication, it is the keeper of a healthy culture and the way to ensure you deliver what you promise.

Key principles from this chapter

- The Visual Factory approach to organisational management is focused on accountability, delivery, transparency and collaboration.
- It is anchored around a disciplined and focused weekly briefing.
- Implemented effectively, the Visual Factory approach can transform culture, performance and innovative capability.
- The key principles are: Membership – the right people in the room; Timekeeping – you start and end on time; Collaboration – all functions have equal status; Vital Few points of data; Accountability and Fairness; Overview of the whole value chain; No speeches, presentations or printouts!

How to implement the principles

- Establish a weekly performance briefing, time-limited and focused, honouring the key principles of the Visual Factory.
- Maintain discipline to avoid discussion creep, information overload or other examples of diluting the core principles of the Visual Factory.

- Reset the core data periodically.
- Ensure fairness and respect for all disciplines. No one is too junior to have their say; no function is 'just a cost base'.

Chapter 8
Complexity Reduction

In my time at LEGO, I often had direct disagreements with head of marketing Mads Nipper. In the rescue and recovery period, 2004–06, I was pushing for a standard operating model across the group. Mads was concerned that if we became too standardised in our approach, LEGO could become a commodity and the business could lose its innovative flair. I understood the point; mine was that we needed the operating model as a foundation for innovation. I still wanted his support, but I didn't get it.

'I'm not going to endorse something I don't understand,' he explained. 'I'm not going to stand in a town hall meeting and be a proponent of something that I can't even explain what it is.'

I was filled with frustration – and also, admiration. It can sometimes take courage, in management, especially in senior executive positions, to admit that you don't understand something. Many businesses would be better-run if more executives displayed this level of integrity. It meant that we could have an honest and realistic conversation. Our relationship was essential to the recovery of the business, as I shall discuss further in this and later chapters. It is a healthy discipline to push for clarity, for detail, for explanation; even if you have a fairly good general grasp of the matter, it will generally help you to know in more detail how it is going to work.

Mads and I resolved our differences on this and other matters, and his candour helped. Too many executives, often out of pride, are reluctant to admit that they are making decisions on operations the workings of which they have only a vague working knowledge of – or in some cases, none at all.

Closely linked to this problem is a tendency for 'complexity creep' in any human organisation. New initiatives, new layers of management, new departments, complex new products with insufficient market research, high leverage and fancy financial instruments tend to increase the complexity of management – and in an exponential, not a linear fashion. If it is at all possible, always reduce complexity. If you are adding complexity, the gains have to be worth the considerable extra managerial time and expertise necessary to oversee everything. At Wellcome, we reduced the number of blister sizes in packs for pharmaceutical products from ten to two. There were only gains as a result of this simplification.

Complexity Reduction

Excessive complexity can kill a business. Some of the most spectacular, and economically damaging, business collapses in the first few decades of the twenty-first century arose in businesses with multiple contracts, complex global interactions and opaque accounts. Enron, Lehman Brothers, Carillion, Wirecard and Greensill Capital are all examples from the period 2000–21. In each of these cases, it is highly likely that hubris and pride were significant factors, as senior executives, board members, auditors, regulators and others – all no doubt highly educated and intelligent folk – were reluctant to admit openly that they did not really understand what was going on in the business's operations. Reassuring soundbites and misleading financial figures were hiding all manner of business risk. Financial wrongdoing was a factor in some of those cases, so individuals will have been deliberately hiding information; nonetheless, generally the opacity and complex nature of the enterprises were likely to have been contributory factors to the crisis.

Even in a toy company, with a relatively straightforward operational supply chain and nothing in the way of financial engineering, complexity can creep in. It has to be managed out. A healthy culture is one of continual improvement: always asking why? until you get an answer, and can take the proper corrective action. At LEGO, we adopted the principle of 'the Vital Few' metrics and we focused on those. This is a simple discipline to conceive but can be tough to stick to. It requires always going back to core operating requirements and the need to 'Deliver What We Promise'. Does this metric help us do that? Measurement is only ever a means to an end.

Lesson from LEGO

At LEGO, a process of radical simplification, featuring a reduction of components, formed a key part of the rescue and turnaround. At its peak in the period 2003–05, there were around 14,500 unique components being manufactured, in line with the strategy of diversification and innovation that had been in operation since the mid-1990s. As well as being costly, the proliferation sometimes worked against the consumer's desires, as there was a lower proportion of interchangeable, universal bricks. Close cooperation between myself as head of supply chain and Mads Nipper, head of marketing, helped release innovative flair leading to successful new designs, imaginative repurposing of common components and simultaneously improved operational efficiency.

There was a clear link between the excessive number of components and the supply problems. At times during the period of crisis, we couldn't guarantee delivery. At one meeting that I attended with representatives of a retailer, one of them had a copy of a standard LEGO base plate, measuring 20 by 20cm. He flung it across the smooth table top towards me and said: 'I'm 45 years old. I used to use this in my LEGO play when I was five. This is component number 626. You have had this in your portfolio for 40 years. Can you tell me how you can run out of this?'

This was a defining moment. Another came the first time I met the buyer from a major retailer, who said to me: 'Can you tell me why I should stock LEGO instead of dog food – where the profit margin is higher and they can actually deliver?'

The colossal number of individual components was a single data point, but a revealing one, when set alongside the mismatches between supply and demand, the failed innovations and the plummeting financial figures. The complexity and cost were being incurred for a negative financial return. Was this an operational nightmare, a failure of strategy, weakness in design and innovation or a lack of ability in the marketing function? The emerging reality those of us in the leadership team discovered was that it was a combination of all of these. This is how wicked problems often emerge in businesses and why a coordinated response is essential. Reducing complexity can be, ironically, a complex task – but you only have to go through the toughest parts once in order to create a more manageable and effective business.

How much complexity is enough?

In earlier chapters, I have described how the strategy went awry at LEGO, with too much diversification and brand stretch; also, how the supply chain was dysfunctional and not adequately supported by the sales and marketing function, or by sufficient consumer research. It was obvious to me, in part because of my training in the strict protocols of the pharmaceutical industry, that these inter-related problems were exacerbated by too much complexity; a profusion of designs and initiatives, too many of which were losing money.

Between 1993 and 2004, the number of components doubled. The justifications were that new products were needed to compete in the marketplace and that the marginal cost of a new mould was low. When you're making profits, such arguments can appear to be sufficient – and trying to measure the exact cost of adding complexity in a business is nigh on impossible. But we had plunged sharply into heavy losses in 2003 and 2004, imperilling the very future of the company. More rigorous enquiry was needed.

In the discussions that followed, among the arguments we put forward from the operations side were that the sheer number of components led to complexity and cost, and that the business faced a pressing need to rationalise the offerings and ensure we move to producing a higher proportion of interchangeable bricks that could be used for more than one model. This provoked some push-back and debate. Some designers felt their creative freedom, central to the continual reinvention that an innovative toy company needs, was being overly restrained. Was there a risk that reducing costs and consumer choice could become a vicious circle; diminishing the offerings, reducing the potential for excitement among our consumers and for growth? This argument had some merit superficially, but it missed the point that with LEGO products, it is the consumer who completes the creations, not us. The greater the proportion of interchangeable, universal bricks, the more options for different models the users had. This led to the counter-intuitive realisation that reducing the range of components could actually increase the building options for an inventive user engaged in creative play.

In practice, the designers devised ingenious repurposing of common bricks to build up models that, when finished, looked highly bespoke and unique. On the pictures of the boxes in a retail outlet, the models of *Star Wars* spacecraft, fire stations or sports cars appear to be highly individual, but many contain a surprising number of standard bricks, in cleverly designed configurations. On display at the central train station in Leeds, England, for example, is a life-size model of a racing cyclist on his bicycle, constructed almost entirely from standard rectangular and square LEGO bricks. A standard 3 x 2 flat brick can form the roof of a car or van. The most brilliant LEGO constructions are co-creations between the company's designers and consumers. In LEGO's own stores, there is a 'Pick a Brick' or 'Pick and Build' section, where users can fill a container with a variety of common bricks. These are highly popular. We borrowed from the DIY retail sector the concept of the 'white paint' – a home improvements store will never run out of white paint. For us, the equivalent was the basic LEGO building products; a lesson vividly brought home to me early in my tenure at LEGO by the retailer who flung a standard base plate across the table to me in a meeting and asked how we could have run out of such a basic piece.

Another crucial consideration was serviceability: when we designed a product with a lot of common parts, it was easier to service when the market runs away, we would have parts in stock, because they're common – and it also becomes easier to shut a product down when it doesn't take off. We needed to curb some costs, but cost-cutting was not the strategic objective. Reducing the number of components meant that excess manufacturing inventory fell dramatically, excess inventory of finished goods fell dramatically, discounting at retailers also fell; all while expanding the creative options for the LEGO fan and restoring the centrality of creative play. There were no downsides, only gains.

Nonetheless aspects of the debate were nuanced and at times there was tension. Designers were right to voice their concerns and to engage in the debate, and without their input, there was a risk of cutting the wrong components. The only way to effect progress was through conversations – deep, frequent conversations, backed up with hard data: not only on cost, but on revenue; and not only quantitative data, but qualitative, taking into account feedback from loyal users as to how we had lost our way by reducing the element of creative play. Mads Nipper, as head of marketing and innovation, was instrumental in these dialogues. As someone with knowledge of design and marketing, he helped me make the case. In an interview for this book, he recalls: 'Everyone agreed that reduction, complexity reduction in our value chain needed to happen . . . . Everyone in the design population, and marketing population, everyone in GIM [Global Innovation and Marketing] at the time, in PMD [Products and Marketing Division] later, firmly believed that design variation, detail, play value, ability to create novelty, needed a lot of components, colours, shapes, so complexity was needed, and it was easy at the time, that those special, stupid elements from Galidor, Jack Stone and so on, everyone agreed that they needed to die. But there had always been a discussion: what is the frame for new elements you could make? That was institutionalised already. So that was not the biggest topic because it was almost personalised, that Bali wanted it too low. And they used me as a wave breaker, saying you've got to talk some sense into these guys.'

A telling moment came when we were able to demonstrate to the wider team that there were no fewer than six mini figures of chefs; another when there were two facial expressions on two separate components which looked almost identical. One of the earliest decisions was to reduce the number of colours. Further progress was enabled by Mads Nipper and myself moving the discussion away from an annual debate over numbers towards a deeper qualitative discussion about quality of the play experience and the impact on the supply chain. Mads produced a matrix mapping design value against value chain complexity. While I do not agree that complexity in the supply chain can be accurately measured, this worked at a conceptual level because it meant that any increase in complexity had to be justified by a commensurate improvement to design quality, the play experience and potential for business growth.

I understand that I was seen as 'the bad guy' – and around this time I came to be known as 'Dr No'. For the record, however, I did not always say 'no'. For example, Mads Nipper and his team made a strong case that components should be grouped into numbered bags, so that a child could have 'little victories' in their play – being able to run in to Mum and say that they had completed a little car, for example, before going on to finish the rest of the set. Feedback from consumers had informed this input. I could see how this would enrich the play experience and so we agreed, even though it added to complexity in the supply chain.

As Mads describes it to me in an interview for this book: 'You never got exactly what you wanted and I never got exactly what I wanted, but we ended up with something that always made a fantastic novelty assortment, and something that also enabled us to have an efficient value chain.'

The two of us had frequent, in-depth discussions, and many arguments, throughout this period. But while we often disagreed, it was only ever about means, not ends: we were prepared to compromise where necessary and we were united in commitment to the company's survival and growth. What was best for the company came first. Tension, often leading to creative tension, marked this relationship and this phase of the recovery. Our relationship had to work, something I will discuss further in Chapter 13.

Summary

There is quite enough complexity in business, as in life, without adding to it. Some of the biggest mistakes in management come from taking on too many conflicting tasks, not having enough time for each and/or not fully understanding the context or the requirements.

Keeping simple what you can keep simple is absolutely central to the approach of Deliver What You Promise. If you don't know, say you don't know. If you don't understand everything, ask questions to fill the gaps in your knowledge. If the answers are not available, or insufficient, don't fill in the gaps with guesswork, wherever possible. If it is essential to proceed with insufficient knowledge, at least be aware of any gaps in intelligence. A proposal that adds complexity to a product range or to operations or organisational structure has to be justified by significant extra opportunities and revenues. Counter-intuitively, simplification of product ranges and production processes can at times boost innovative potential as well as operating efficiency, as we demonstrated at LEGO.

My motto when I became CEO at LEGO was: 'Simplify to Grow', as I shall discuss in later chapters. Many find this a useful operating principle as executives.

Key principles from this chapter

- Too much complexity can kill a business; some of the most significant corporate collapses of recent decades featured highly complex structures and opaque reporting.
- It requires integrity and honesty to admit that you do not understand something; such humility is generally a managerial strength.
- Reducing complexity tends to boost transparency and efficiency; counter-intuitively, it can boost flexibility and innovative capacity also.

- Adding to complexity must have a compelling case, in terms of opportunities.

How to implement the principles

- Subject any proposal that adds complexity to a rigorous analysis of potential benefits, combined with an understanding of how it will add to demands upon managers and the company's resources.
- Try to identify ways in which a company's operations can be made simpler, clearer and more understandable; if you do, it is likely that such an exercise will have multiple benefits.
- Despite the potential for multiple benefits, reducing complexity can come with risks, like any managerial exercise. If others push back against a simplification programme, treat them with respect and engage in meaningful conversations.

Chapter 9
Leadership Can Emerge Anywhere

'I think I may get fired today,' I told my wife Sati via my mobile phone, as I made the short walk from my hotel to the LEGO headquarters in Billund, Denmark, one morning in 2005, on my way to a crucial executive meeting. All walks in Billund are short. The town where the toy firm has its headquarters was a small farming village in the 1930s when Ole Kirk Kristiansen founded his business, initially making wooden implements and then toys for local people. By the twenty-first century the large modern HQ with its visitor centre dominated the town.

So, I had little time to gather my thoughts. This was a pivotal moment in the turnaround and I had stayed awake until 4am the night before in order to finalise my presentation. I had some tough messages to tell my colleagues. In effect they were demands, because our perspective from supply was that the business could not survive without the reforms we were requesting. Matters had built up to a crisis point, not just for the supply chain, but for the prospects of the business. Many of the dysfunctions in the North American operations, and the strategic errors with failed products and brand stretch, described in earlier chapters, combined in such a way as to threaten the viability of the entire firm. Operationally, we were not delivering what we were promising. Strategically, we were not always promising what the market wanted. But the designers, engineers and many of the products were world-class and the brand was loved around the world – the potential was enormous.

Leadership involves management and management involves leadership

A business cannot function if every unit or department has its own strategy and there is insufficient cooperation. But it cannot function either if the function heads are overly passive, fail to take the initiative and show leadership, just waiting for the senior executive team for every decision.

A central piece of learning from my long career is this: that there is more management in leadership roles, and more leadership in management roles, than many seem to appreciate. Chapter 3 includes a discussion on the importance of management in leading executive roles: how the C-suite should have a strong grasp of operational reality and not be too far above the organisation (*see also* pages 47–71). Norlys CEO Niels Duedahl expressed this perfectly when he described the executive's need to know 20 per cent of operational detail and how 'believing you can do the role with just 2 per cent – that's not possible'.

This chapter describes some of the leadership capabilities a business manager needs to possess. It means standing up for the function you represent, while still being able to forge partnerships with other functions. It means speaking truth to power. It means harnessing the engagement of your team. The distinction between leadership and management can be helpful, but only up to a point: the two roles are conjoined. Leaders have to be able to manage; and managers lead.

During a turnaround, a leader has to be very directive. Headlines in the business sections of news media tend to highlight the cuts: to personnel, of loss-making products, certain factories and offices. Every bit as important, however, are those units and people who need retaining; products and services that need reinvigorating, or staff whose morale and sense of purpose needs restoring. This was true at LEGO during its rescue and recovery. CEO Jørgen Vig Knudstorp got the big calls right: he understood both the parts, and the whole, and he did not slash and burn. There were painful changes deemed necessary, however – especially when he streamlined the management team in September 2005, a decision over which he later confided he had shed tears.

I was one of two survivors from a cull of seven executives in supply and manufacturing. Some people's nerves were shaken by the crisis. There was a lot of grieving, emotions were raw. We had never seen a mass firing before. I was grieving too, over the loss of close colleagues. There were conversations at the water cooler about who would be next and 'Could it be me?' It was a time of both great promise and considerable risk as the survival of the company was in the balance. We had to strike the right balance between accountability and performance-management on the one hand and support and nurture for employees on the other.

I decided I had to take a lead. Morale was not devastated, but it had clearly been shaken. I wrote to my team, a missive which I called the 'Letter to the New Organisation', describing the culture of transparency and performance that we were instilling; a policy of 'Deliver What We Promise'. Reading it again some 15 years later, I think it reads well.

The emotional and logistical content were both prominent. If anything, the messages on emotional engagement were the stronger. This emphasis was important, because people were in shock. After the cull of senior managers on the supply side, even those most supportive of the move from a business point of view would have felt some fear; the fear that no one's job was safe. Such a psychological earthquake demands a leadership response that is sensitive as well as decisive – not a combination that is easy to strike.

I set out the need to focus on the supply side, to work backwards from what the customer needed. I made a commitment to get my own hands dirty and fix what needed to be fixed. The letter also reminded members of my team of the affection for the toys that we were producing for families around the world and that we were presented with an opportunity to save and restore to glory a famous and much-loved brand.

I am not claiming I got everything right, by any means. Progress in business, as in life, tends to be uneven. But the team did rally, building on the foundations we had already built, which turned out to be strong enough to support renewed, indeed exceptional, growth, continuing for more than 15 years at the time of writing and exceeding expectations.

Time for candour: winning the point

The meeting on that memorable morning in Billund – held shortly before the cull of senior managers – had to confront the need to improve data, transparency and communication right across the business and a much better matching of demand and supply. I was not certain that my tough message would be welcomed, or that I would receive sufficient support. The people resisting requests for more transparency would not have seen themselves as being obstructive or unprofessional; rather, it was a culture clash. Organisational cultures grow up over years and within large, complex businesses each department will have its own culture – which is not a problem, as long as they learn to cooperate.

As we began introducing more transparency and requesting data, there was a clash of perception. The approach to planning and logistics that we had started in the North American operations, later spread throughout the group, emphasised the importance of clear data across the value chain, understanding the whole organisation as an ecosystem. From this perspective, it was essential to have relevant information from the manufacturing side to help us balance supply and demand. To some in Denmark, however, we seemed to come across as intrusive: 'They're telling us how to do our job' – or our requests for data were seen as just bureaucracy. I could understand this, although it was frustrating. It was sometimes not possible even to have access to basic information, such as how many moulds there were. In sales, some people felt that we should simply make what they ordered – but our response was that we had been doing that and it was leading to too much waste so the negotiations were difficult. Resistance that we encountered even ran to the extent of people not giving me data because they felt it was being used against them. I was accused of 'seeing ghosts' when I warned of the data not being clean enough prior to implementation of the new information system. Danish culture favours consensus – which can be a tremendous asset, but can become a liability in a crisis when fast actions and decisions are necessary. But I had some allies, including individuals who had experience in data cleansing.

Much success in business derives from being disciplined in some relatively unglamorous tasks.

One of my fellow planners, an American lady and an excellent professional, had come over to Billund to help with introducing the reforms. Even though we had the backing of Jørgen Vig Knudstorp, she and I encountered resistance: what we had expected to be a process of implementation became a discussion over the merits of the new system – something we had reason to believe had been settled. At one point my American colleague even threatened to give up and return over the Atlantic. We gave the Danish team some time to devise a plan while we left the room – upon our return, they had produced a programme that would have taken several weeks. They didn't get it. The business was burning, we needed changes within five days. Production lines were idle and we weren't meeting demand.

As I walked from the hotel to the HQ, I knew that the problem was systemic, not solely within our department. I decided that, if I was going to be scapegoated anyway, there was little harm in being honest and forthright in my assessment. I would rather get fired for being honest than collude with a state of denial and go down with the ship, so after my presentation I asked Jørgen directly if he could ask the salespeople either side of him to explain why the demand could not be met as no manufacturing organisation could supply such huge and unpredictable variance.

As it turned out, this meeting was a turning point in the way in which senior management saw the demand and supply issue. I had won another battle. This was a leadership role, which is distinct from a strategic role. The two are often taken to be synonyms, but in this chapter, I make what I believe to be an important distinction: a business needs a single strategy. Moreover, it is one that needs to be updated and altered continually. But – and this is a big but – this does not mean that internal leaders – function heads and other managers – are subservient and meek. You need to lead; to have the capacity to speak truth to power. This type of leadership within a management role requires an approximately equal blend of assertiveness and cooperation, geared towards delivering the strategy, which in turn is geared towards pleasing the ultimate consumers of your products or services. A business is a complex organism. In practice, the head of each specialist function needs simultaneously to defend the interests of that function and collaborate closely with others in a state of delicate balance and creative tension.

Encouraging leadership within the firm

Earlier chapters, in particular Chapter 5 (*see also* pages 89–114), describe the strategic errors prior to the appointment of Jørgen Vig Knudstorp as CEO of LEGO in 2004. He oversaw an effective strategic renewal – and he did so while understanding the contribution of the different functions and ensuring a good grasp of operational fundamentals. A CEO cannot manage each function directly; he or she has to encourage leadership within the firm. As described, the operational and strategic problems were so intertwined that they had to be addressed in parallel, not sequentially.

Jørgen had studied and come to understand both the strength of the brand and the weakness of the business as it was in 2004. He looked at potential as well as profit margins, having noted that no one had properly kept an eye on complexity of operations during the push for growth and diversification in the 1990s and early 2000s. He picked up that the core fanbase felt that the company had lost its way and sought to re-engage their enthusiasm.

Streamlining a business has to be done with care. During an emergency rescue phase of a company, thoughtless cutting of costs can make matters worse because cutting the wrong costs impairs the customer experience or harms the potential to attract new customers. While it is tempting simply to close the loss-making products and divisions, even this can be a mistake because today's loss-makers can be tomorrow's cash cows with better management. Above all, the products need to support the core vision, the customer's understanding of what the brand ought to offer. Jørgen was aware of all this and was thorough in his analysis. He did not panic and took the time to understand the business, the market and the situation. In his push for greater focus and discipline, I was a natural ally. For months I had been pushing my team to deliver what we promised, to reduce the unnecessary complexity that had been so much of a problem at the time that I had joined. He saw in me someone who was already reforming operations in the way that would support his vision for the company.

Jørgen was not an 'ivory tower' strategist, he took a close interest in operations. In the early part of the turnaround he wanted an action plan, not a strategy – the 'Manage for Cash' phase. In a similar way, my priority when joining the US was to fix matters operationally as a matter of urgency. As part of his preparation for the CEO role, Jørgen asked probing questions of senior managers in order to understand the business fully. His research was thorough and professional. Quite early in his tenure as CEO he was intrigued by the Demand & Operations Planning system that we had introduced in the US. He invited me over to Denmark and asked me to explain how it worked and why it was important. I convinced him of the importance of such a system and in 2004 I was appointed to my first group-level role, as head of planning and logistics. This was a vote of confidence in me and the US team and enabled us to introduce our ways of working to the business as a whole. His thorough preparation helped him make the big calls correctly and support operations effectively – such as at the key meeting in Billund, where the problems were laid bare.

The results are in . . .

As we began to implement the reforms, around reduced components, better data on product profitability, capacity, demand and product differentiation, the benefits started to become clear. Reducing the component number on its own delivered multiple benefits (*see also* Chapter 8, pages 148–154). It's rare in business management that implementing a reform surprises you on the upside: that the benefits are bigger, and come sooner, than expected. Operationally, we had better control of costs, greater serviceability of components and better ability to match supply to demand. In terms of sales, they started to head upwards as early as 2005, a short way into the turnaround. Relaunches of LEGO City, DUPLO, TECHNIC and MINDSTORMS resulted in sales growth. Innovation, far from being stunted as operations exerted greater influence within the company, became highly imaginative.

During the crucial period of September to December 2005, however, there was still much anxiety. For all their promise, there was no guarantee that the changes we had been making would end the sequence of heavy financial losses from the two previous years. The run-up to Christmas is obviously a crucial period for any toy firm. Demand was rising but the twin challenges for us were being able to meet the demand without a drop in quality and *knowing* we could meet that demand – having accurate data across the supply chain. At this point, I was holding daily meetings with my people. Creating transparency and holding people accountable was a big piece of the initiative. It wasn't until the third week of October that we felt confident about meeting an ambitious target for Christmas demand.

We did it! Sales beat expectations. Supply met demand. Quality was there. Customers were happy. And for the first time in three years, the company posted a profit at year-end 2005. From the point of view of those of us responsible for the supply chain, the changes we had introduced visibly made a decisive contribution. We began to lose the tag 'Assholes INC' (it took years to lose it completely!) and established credibility. The phrase I used was: 'We are an equal partner around the table'.

Summary

Leadership is often equated with strategy. This book describes the more nuanced and complex reality: each function does not have its own strategy – it has to support the firm's purpose and strategy – but each function head does need to display leadership abilities: the ability to inspire the team, negotiate on behalf of them; to display an appropriate blend of assertiveness and collaborative ability. Leadership is part of what you do as a manager and any sustained improvement in performance involves an act of leadership. A CEO needs simultaneously to ensure direction around a coherent strategy and to nurture appropriate leadership abilities within the managerial population.

Key principles from this chapter

- Operational managers need leadership ability. They need to be able to take the initiative where they see problems that run across the business that need addressing, and they need to instil pride, purpose and direction in their team, as well as representing their interests internally.
- Managers need to forge partnerships with other functional heads within the business.
- In a business turnaround, it is as important to identify parts of the business that need to be retained and restored as it is to make cuts – identifying those units, products and services that have a future may require detailed analysis.

How to implement the principles

- Speak truth to power. Generally, if you see something is wrong, or needs saying, that might upset or appear inconvenient to colleagues or the most senior executive, it is still better to say it.

Deliver What You Promise

- Stay calm, be factual – the way in which you communicate your position, or highlight inconvenient truths, is important. Be respectful to others and not accusing; state the facts calmly and present an honest position, setting out credible options.
- Attend to morale, purpose and direction, as well as tasks and targets: emotions are always involved.

Chapter 10
Don't Automate Everything

There is an understandable – but fatal – impulse among many in business to automate everything and measure everything. Neither is necessary nor desirable. Businesses exist to serve people, otherwise they have no function. All machines and measurements are means to that end. Hence, I always insisted on the 'Vital Few' points of data – those which actually help us achieve the commercial objectives of delighting the consumer (*see also* Chapter 7 on the Visual Factory, pages 127–144). I have always resisted complexification, preferring to keep simple those things that can be kept simple, because life is complicated enough. And you cannot measure complexity – there are too many variables and precious few constants. The science, craft and art of management need to be held in some kind of balance – moreover, it is in part an empirical science, not always a precise one: the most effective discipline is to measure those vital few pieces of information that enable you to achieve. We are living in a digital economy and one that is inevitably becoming more digital, given the rise of platform-based business models such as Airbnb and Uber, respectively a holiday and transport company that do not own properties or vehicles but instead use digital connections to link providers and consumers. Data is often described as 'the new gold', which has an element of truth but which, like most mantras, is a simplification. And data is only useful to a business if it is a) relevant and b) clean.

Automating a bad system thoughtlessly can result in simply doing the wrong things more quickly. Look! We've irritated and inconvenienced the customers even more swiftly than we used to! As noted earlier in Chapter 1, when consumers bring forward requests or complaints it should not be too difficult for them to get through to a person who can empathise and provide the right kind of advice and support. This is especially the case where the emotional bond between the individual and the product is likely to be strong, as is the case with LEGO, where we always ensured there were well-trained people to respond to questions and complaints from LEGO users. It is common to automate consumer responses and reviews, which can yield important information, but if you pick up some one-star reviews because you've failed to deliver, gathering the information is not enough. The important point is: Have you apologised and offered to fix the problems?

At operational level, there may be more scope for automation and streamlining processes, but it still has to be done with care. I would often say at LEGO that moulding had to be efficient and packing had to be effective. On moulding, the mantra was 'Lean'; on packing, the mantra was 'Agile'. For a similar reason, we learned to be highly selective about which parts of the process were suitable for automation. Obviously, artificial intelligence systems have developed rapidly both during my stay at LEGO and since, but this does not mean that automation should be maximised.

This is especially the case in a highly volatile and unpredictable market like toys. I had to deal with this issue throughout my time at LEGO: young engineers would come in and naturally want to make a contribution, and improving efficiency through automation is one way of doing this, but I often had to educate people around the need to look at the business needs and to understand the whole of the value chain, and the impact of incentives and hence behaviour. For example, from 2003–04, I was being persuaded to automate data capture on the packing lines. What we discovered was that the packing personnel were incentivised on how many bricks per minute they were packing without regard for inventory in the warehouse or retailer needs. This in turn led to people in packing pushing for a longer run, to improve their rate of bricks packed per minute, rather than follow demand. The request was for the data to be captured automatically, but I challenged this, saying that it was the wrong measure to be monitoring, and that the incentives created were perverse. Yet this type of request – to automate without sufficient consideration to the impact – continued to revisit me until my retirement from an executive role.

Value drivers and cost drivers

Key to understanding how a commercial operation functions is to understand the drivers of value, and the drivers of cost, in some depth and to understand them together. Being lean and curbing costs is often described as essential in supply chains, but this is too narrow a focus. Yes, cost reduction and improvements to efficiency and productivity are important and necessary, but only when conducted as part of understanding of the impact on the full value chain, otherwise they can be counter-productive. In extreme cases, they can even become a self-defeating compulsion, especially where incentives are not aligned with what the company needs to do to meet consumers' and retailers' needs. For example, when I joined LEGO in the US in 2003–04, our business was haemorrhaging cash, retailers were screaming at us and we could not supply adequately – serious dysfunctions. One of the misaligned incentives causing or exacerbating some of these problems was encouraging a form of cost-cutting that was a false economy. Our moulds were worn and constantly breaking down, requiring shutting down the machine and making repairs, causing interruption in supply. It transpired that the person responsible for ordering new moulds was incentivised to reduce costs and he did this by not ordering replacement moulds and keeping old ones beyond their useful life. Yet the bonus scheme at the time rewarded him for doing this. He was getting A++ in appraisals and receiving bonuses while effectively harming value for the company by cutting the wrong cost.

My challenging of some approaches to automating certain processes resulted in some colleagues I have worked with mistakenly assuming I had a certain prejudice against automation. This is not the case – it is a process that can add considerable value. My point – which I hope I have made sufficiently clear during my career – is to be crystal clear about *what* you were automating; *why*; and how the process contributes to the overall value chain. Deploying the latest digital connectivity does not guarantee you have a modern, agile and high-performing business, in the same way that owning a superbly engineered car won't guarantee that you will be a great driver.

Information systems not working

The point about automation can be extended to introduction of new technology generally. One of the commonest mistakes when introducing IT systems across a business is to treat it as solely or primarily a technical exercise, with organisational and people-management matters relegated to the fringes. In practice, it is first and foremost a cultural and behavioural challenge. There is a considerable amount of literature showing that failures in implementing new systems are commonly linked to weaknesses in people-management and communication. Findings from a five-year study published in *Harvard Business Review* in August 2020 into advanced technological systems, such as artificial intelligence, found that:

> *Our key takeaway is counterintuitive. Competing in the age of AI is not about being technology-driven per se – it's a question of new organizational structures that use technology to bring out the best in people. The secret to making this work, we learned, is the business model itself, where machines and humans are integrated to complement each other. Machines do repetitive and automated tasks and will always be more precise and faster. However, those uniquely human skills of creativity, care, intuition, adaptability, and innovation are increasingly imperative to success.*[14]

This was equally true in 2004 at LEGO, when the major challenge was around cleaning the data and ensuring it was relevant, while a new Systems Applications and Products

(SAP) system was being introduced (*see also* Chapter 9, pages 164–6). The point about getting the human systems right first is a timeless insight into all technologies, not just Artificial Intelligence (AI) and information technology. If you buy a system from a reputable supplier like SAP, the kit will work fine: what determines a successful implementation is the quality and relevance of the data, how people are using it and how effectively they are collaborating. This is where the Visual Factory helped, but unfortunately some legacy issues around the LEGO culture did not.

These points reinforce the idea of management being art, craft and science in equal measure – something that many entrepreneurs grasp more readily than some investors. It isn't only science; or perhaps more accurately, it includes empirical science as well as measurement and data. The desire for measurement is understandable – and I completely agree that accurate data is essential where relevant, so that you are dealing with facts rather than assumptions – but not everything can be measured. This is especially the case in the start-up phase, as Tony Fadell, inventor of the iPod and founder of NEST, points out in an interview for this book: 'Data people want a report with data. Everyone wants a calculation to show that it's going to work. There's opinion-based decision-making versus vision-based decision-making. There is a tendency to turn it into data-based decision-making. But you will never get data until you ship. At 2.0 and 3.0 it can be much more data-driven, or data plus intuition, but at 1.0 it can't be. We don't know – but we judge that the world is moving this way, and we're not going to get it wrong forever. This is the trend. You learn by doing and failing, and optimising and trying again. Almost everyone wants data-driven analysis to cover their ass and they want a bonus, but at the start it's not possible.'

Summary

The digital revolution is real, it is ongoing. It holds much potential, in common with all technological breakthroughs. In the social and political world, there are concerns over the handling of personal data by digital companies and the 'echo chambers' of extreme groups on social media. Against that, there are multiple ways in which digital change brings people together in socially beneficial ways. Similarly, in business, digital systems can be tremendously empowering – but only if the human systems are also working well. The technology is just the car: you are the driver.

Key principles from this chapter

- Technology is a means to an end; it is essential to get the human systems right as a first priority.
- Deploying the most advanced technology and digital systems does not guarantee greater effectiveness, in the

same way that having the best car doesn't make you the best driver.

- Automating a process without sufficient consideration to how it fits into the whole value chain can result in simply doing the wrong things more quickly.

How to implement the principles

- Always look at how a new technology – of whatever kind – fits into the overall value chain and the human system, when assessing how to deploy it.
- Not everything can be monitored and measured with precision – it often helps to have a blend of data, qualitative insights and judgement.
- Attention may need to be paid to financial incentives tied to activities that are candidates for automation.
- Try to ensure it is easy for consumers with genuine requests or complaints to be able to talk with a well-trained adviser who can help them directly.

Chapter 11
A Sense of Purpose Ensures Performance

If there is a unifying theme that runs through the chapters of this book, it is breaking down barriers and connecting people: listening to the Beatles with my English friends as a schoolboy, or going to the pub when we were old enough, breaking the rumoured racial bar; encouraging collaboration across business disciplines in my career, overcoming prejudice, engaging individuals regarded as junior or in 'menial' tasks, seeing the enterprise as an organism of interdependent parts, not a static set of departments.

The prejudice I have encountered as a British Asian making my way in European society was one challenge, of which there is increasing awareness. A less obvious bias that caused immense frustration in my working life as a supply-chain specialist has been an ivory tower mentality. This regards strategy, innovation, design and branding as 'sexy' or 'value-adding'; and operations, supply and logistics as transactional or subservient. This hierarchy is arbitrary and unhelpful. A supply chain is a way of connecting people. It is not a mere cost base – a misleading notion fashionable for a while in management circles and an attitude that can still be encountered. It can lead to inappropriate or poorly planned outsourcing projects and neglect of customer service. Managing the supply chain well requires intellect and creativity. Moreover, it is at the heart of delivering what you promise.

Allied to this concept is an understanding of the importance of purpose and harnessing the skills, endeavours and commitment of all within the enterprise. This chapter focuses on this crucial dimension and the need for honest conversations and effective negotiation to support it. For a business to be effective, most of the colleagues, and certainly the key functional heads, need to be genuinely committed to its success, rather than be pursuing ego-fuelled projects or just passing time while registering a certain employer on their CV.

Teamwork, communication and operational excellence

A most vivid and telling example of the importance of purpose and how the operational and relational aspects of business are inextricably linked – effectively one and the same – came in the working relationship between myself and Mads Nipper, LEGO's head of marketing. We had different professional backgrounds, often very different perspectives, but were each expert and equally committed to the success of the company.

Without working very hard at our relationship, it may have proved impossible for us to resolve major operational matters and deliver the strategy during the crucial turnaround, recovery and growth phases in LEGO, in the period 2005–12. The different mindsets and approaches we took could have resulted in crisis without this intensive effort. We renewed this discussion in interviews I held with Mads in preparation for this book. Even after a few years away from the business, we still have to agree to disagree on some matters, but because we developed a strong partnership, based on mutual respect and open discussion, we resolved the major challenges that we faced at the time. In our interview, Mads says: 'I think the honest truth was that you and I, Bali, fundamentally were running the company. We did not run the very forward-looking strategies, the grand strategies of what would happen – that was to a large extent Jørgen – but in reality, all short-term operations and planning was done by us.'

At LEGO, we worked hard at relationships, recognising them as central to the turnaround and later to sustained performance. We benefited from the intervention of a specialist business coach who worked closely with us. It was notable that some of our colleagues from a finance or operations background were unenthusiastic about the importance of understanding relationships, motives, communication styles and so on. Mads and I, by contrast, were keen students. Recalling our past disagreements in conversation, as part of the preparation for this book, yielded what I hope are helpful observations on how the operational and the relational are inextricably linked.

Mads and I have different professional backgrounds and, as a result, differing priorities and mindsets. I am a supply-chain specialist, he is a marketer. In the years of recovery from crisis, we sometimes had different perspectives. Issues that I raised to improve operational efficiency jarred with him as a creative dedicated to ensuring that LEGO remained at the cutting edge of toy design. Mads describes the problems he had with some of my proposals as 'stones in the shoe', but also how the discussions facilitated by a business coach helped. He recalls a particular disagreement following my suggestion that LEGO becomes 'the Toyota of the toy industry'. My ambition was to learn from the Japanese car-maker because not only did it have exceptional commitment to quality, teamwork and continual improvement, but it had a modular design system, in which the same chassis or axle could be used for more than one model – in the same way that I wanted to maximise multiple uses of core LEGO components.

But Mads saw things differently. He recalls: 'That was tough for me because I saw Toyota as a very well-run commodity product company. It was high-quality but absolutely no emotions, no desirability. That was for those people who just want transportation. And I said, "That's not what LEGO is about. LEGO is about excitement; it's the world's best play experience. How can they even make the analogy?" And I think you and I had a session where I mentioned that to you. I said: "This is really painful for me, because I feel we are not on the same page." And then you explained to me what you meant. You were not aspiring to be the same kind of brand, but you were aspiring to take the best out of having a kind of Toyota production system and how can we do that? And I said, "Ah, I get it." So, in that sense the business coach's process was very good at removing some of those stones in the shoe that there were despite an always-present huge mutual respect for each other's professions.'

In his experience, the facilitated sessions greatly strengthened the bond between us, although not all relationships within the senior management team – in part because some did not fully engage with the 'soft stuff'. This underlines the complexity of group work. Mads adds: 'From a coherent team perspective, it [the facilitated groupwork] was not really successful, but for strengthening the relations between the two guys who were the fundamental operational axis of the company it worked exceptionally well. Both you and I, we knew even before that process that both of us were just trying to do what was right for the company.'

In a similar way, he rebelled initially against my push to operationalise the company around a core operating model. Jørgen had approved it. Mads was pushing back. He says: 'I think what happened was a collision of two thinking styles, because I think both you and Jørgen had this, you were saying that this concept of an operating model that says how do we actually operate? What are the fundamentals of how we operate the company? How do we underlie those with processes that are coherent? How do we ensure that the leadership supports that? And so on.'

The fear of Mads, and some others in marketing, was similar to the issue with Toyota: might we become too focused on operational effectiveness and lose the dynamism and inventiveness that LEGO depended upon? Again, we couldn't have resolved the issue without attending to our relationship, as well as the presenting issues.

Mads recalls: 'Even though I found it quite painful at the time, it was actually a really important learning experience for me, and I think the interactions and the friction that especially you and I had was actually absolutely foundational for this to be successful. Because if we had not had it [this discussion], then those frictions would have happened elsewhere. And I still remember saying "I'm not going to endorse something [the operating model] I don't understand. I'm not going to stand in a town hall meeting and be a proponent of something that I can't even explain what it is." You were super annoyed because you were saying "yes, we can explain it". But we can only explain it down to this level. That doesn't do it for me. And I won't communicate something I don't understand.'

Mads felt that if design was being reduced to a process, there would be insufficient emphasis on originality and creativity. He wanted more appreciation of 'the single most important discipline in the company, namely whether we can create fantastic products or not'. I agreed, and many of the points of agreement lay in the detail. To me, a strong operational platform created the foundation for creativity; I wanted to enhance inventiveness, not curb it. Simplifying processes, reducing components and enhancing reliability of the supply chain were initiatives that I championed, that were always intended to liberate designers, not imprison them. The points of difference between us, in the end, were small, but because we had different mindsets reflecting our different professional backgrounds, they had loomed large. Only by working at the relationship, and through in-depth discussions, could we achieve this joint agreement. The out-in-the-open debate that the two of us held prevented greater friction elsewhere in the business, says Mads, which could have become hardened into faction-building and fault-lines within the managerial population.

What is it you really want? The importance of drive

The context of the business, and the leadership quality, are obviously of paramount importance, but a dimension that can be neglected is individual drive. What is the person really striving for? Do they want this company to succeed, or are they treading water, waiting for their next opportunity? Are they pushing for an initiative more because it would look good on the CV than because it would drive sales or operational effectiveness?

In my decade-long working relationship with Mads Nipper we disagreed about much. We disagreed about the extent to which components should be reduced; whether you can plot the decision on a matrix, about the importance of a central operating system. We agreed about much also. What bound us together was a shared ethic: we passionately, genuinely, wanted LEGO to succeed. The arguments were often about means, not ends.

Where I have often seen projects go awry, or misconceived projects, in some cases is where managers lack this essential commitment to the business succeeding. Instead, they have their eye on the next job and are seeking to register a certain experience on their resumé. There is no easy way for senior executives to monitor or handle misaligned ambitions where they are serious and prolonged – and after all, we all have an ego and no one is pure. Rather, it is a matter for general awareness, especially at the recruiting stage.

A Sense of Purpose Ensures Performance

Summary

Alignment of purpose is essential for delivering what you promise. This might sound obvious, but can be difficult in practice because professional perspectives, personalities and short-term interests of different functions can cause misalignments – or appear to, owing to differing vocabularies and culture clashes. Only through deep and honest conversations can the most difficult differences be either resolved or accommodated through compromise. In turn, selection, recruitment and team formation need to be geared towards helping the enterprise deliver what they promise. This is not helped by the arbitrary segregation of business disciplines into supposedly 'hard' and 'soft' issues – something that will be discussed in the next chapter.

Key principles from this chapter

- A supply chain is not primarily a cost base, it is a way of connecting people.
- A shared sense of purpose is essential to deliver what you promise and ensure effective operations and a successful business. It is especially important among key functional heads.
- Differences of culture, of professional background, can cause misunderstandings, but if there is an underlying

191

ethic of helping the enterprise succeed, these can be overcome.

- It is perfectly acceptable for two or more individuals to hold honestly held differences of view over strategy or tactics, and helpful to have a forum in which these can be discussed.

How to implement the principles

- If there is an apparently strong disagreement, it helps to dig deep to discern what the real policy or other differences are.
- An expert facilitator can help resolve differences and improve working relationships. For certain relationships of strategic importance, this may even be essential.
- It is not necessary to seek to 'win' on each point of a difficult negotiation; the overriding objective needs to be ensuring the business as a whole survives and thrives.

Chapter 12
'Hard' and 'Soft' Managerial Issues is a False Distinction

Everything in a company is interconnected. The business as an organism, part of a wider ecosystem, is a better metaphor than a set of structures. This reorientation of understanding of the company as a living entity has profound implications. It means ending the distinction between 'hard' and 'soft' business disciplines and seeing everything as an interconnected whole; business leaders need to fully acknowledge and understand how impaired performance or efficiency often has a psychological root cause – misaligned motives, departmental rivalry, frustrated ambition, poor communication and so on. There is specialist learning within the realms of psychology and group dynamics, but the problem of segregation into 'hard' and 'soft' disciplines is that relational and psychological aspects are often neglected when making decisions about business structure or costs, sometimes with disastrous results. The real business is the people. Factors such as motives, relationships and morale are just as important when considering an outsourcing decision as when designing a leadership development programme or seeking to boost employee engagement. The difficult outsourcing relationship between LEGO and Flextronics (*see also* Chapter 6, pages 120–3) involved a mismatch of business models and a misjudgement (in my opinion) on core competence, but also cultural and relational matters; you cannot disentangle the different categories.

It is common in business to critique what may be a lack of commercial business awareness on the part of specialists in human resources or HR. Often it is a fair and relevant criticism and at times in my executive career I have intervened to encourage a stronger sense of business accountability regarding decisions made by the HR function. The other side of the coin, however, is that many in technical disciplines such as engineering or finance are dismissive of the importance of psychology and human relations, which is a similar and equal error. More than once I have heard such folk say that they want nothing to do with 'namby-pamby HR stuff'. In my experience, this is every bit as wrong-headed as HR specialists not understanding the money-making logic of the firm. We can only deliver in a collaborative way; understanding relationships, personal ambitions and the importance of communications is vital. The operational and the relational sides of a business are closely and inextricably linked. I am a supply-chain specialist. Whenever I have seen efficiency and quality slide in business operations, invariably there is a strong behavioural and emotional content to the underlying factors, such as misguided personal motives or hidden beliefs.

My understanding of this interconnection of the relational and operational has received intellectual backing in recent years – for example, from Yves Morieux, a business adviser for the Boston Consulting Group, who advised us at LEGO. He memorably informed us that if you understand people's goals, resources and constraints, you go a long way towards understanding their behaviour. I have found this to be a valuable guide. He also argues powerfully that dividing the business into 'hard' and 'soft' issues is arbitrary and unhelpful. You cannot separate psychological and operational factors, because ultimately it is people who will deliver for you – or not.

In an eloquent and dazzling TED Talk in 2014, he described how businesses struggle to become more productive and effective and end up becoming complex and bureaucratic. The root cause is the misguided definition of 'hard' and 'soft' matters, he argued.

'The way we organise is based on two pillars. The hard – structure, processes, systems. The soft – feelings, sentiments, interpersonal relationships, traits, personality. And whenever a company reorganises, restructures, reengineers, goes through a cultural transformation program, it chooses these two pillars. Now, we try to refine them, we try to combine them. The real issue is . . . these pillars are obsolete. Everything you read in business books is based either on one or the other or their combination. They are obsolete.'

In the talk, he drew attention to the irony that discussions around the so-called 'hard' areas of management often involve metaphors and proxies instead of describing the real business. He said that when addressing the so-called 'hard' matters: 'You start with strategy, requirements, structures, processes, systems, KPIs [Key Performance Indicators], scorecards, committees, headquarters, hubs, clusters, you name it. I forgot all the metrics, incentives, committees, middle offices and interfaces. You have more complexity. This is the new complexity of business.'[15]

Organisational structure diagrams, reporting lines and reports about the situation are not the real business, they are proxies or descriptions. The real business involves the people and the responsibilities and tasks that they have. He admired the Visual Factory approach to management (*see also* Chapter 7, pages 127–144) when he visited LEGO, because it involved the people in the room who were actually responsible for the tasks, communicating directly with each other about the tasks in hand. I introduced the Visual Factory approach to LEGO, initially at the North American operation, though it subsequently spread throughout the business and has since been adopted at other businesses.

That is not to say that metrics, KPIs never have a role to play, it is to understand that they are an insufficient replacement for more direct forms of accountability and that the false dichotomy between 'hard' and 'soft' matters has tended to encourage a proliferation of these proxies so that discussions become dislocated from reality. This point is similar to the one made in the book *Execution: The Discipline of Getting Things Done* by Ram Charan and Larry Bossidy (*see also* Chapter 3, pages 48–54), where struggling chief executives did not understand operational reality clearly enough. A continual challenge for me as chief operations officer, and later as CEO at LEGO, was to prune back the burgeoning complexity that seems to develop in a long-established successful business, like weeds in an allotment.

Team building: to what purpose?

A further problem with the division of business into 'hard' and 'soft' issues is that it often results in sub-optimal approaches to relationships and team building, as well as business performance and accountability. The problem lies in the separation of the two. Many people have worked in businesses where there is poor or erratic collaboration in their daily working lives – inadequate guidance and feedback, insufficient resources, unrealistic expectations – and then been sent on a 'team-building' away day featuring all kinds of activities from quizzes to outdoor pursuits, only to be sent back into the dysfunctional workplace and expected to perform to a higher standard. This represents an extreme dislocation and it is pretty much doomed to fail. It may even be counterproductive if it raises expectations of greater support but fails to deliver them consistently.

In the course of my career, I became sceptical of the value of many team-building exercises, or at least, activities that are called 'team-building', but are really social. It's possible some managers call social events 'team-building' because then it qualifies as a business expense. If you want to reward people with a fun event, then fine, but it may be better to call it a social event whose aim is unambiguously entertainment, such as ten-pin bowling or go-karting. Real team building involves talking about the real issues, discussing and not avoiding the difficult conversations. Team members may have different perspectives, and will come from different backgrounds, but it is important that you share a sense of purpose and commit to building the underlying trust. You develop the capacity of being able to agree to disagree (*see also* Chapter 11, pages 184–9). Facilitated discussions to improve communication and relationships can help. Most employees want to do a good job and take pride in their work. One of the most empowering and engaging experiences for a team is to collectively deliver what they promise and receive glowing feedback from customers as a result. I have some sympathy with the anonymous banker quoted by Lucy Kellaway in the *Financial Times* in 2011, who said: 'It's that time of year again when spring has sprung and our bosses still think that team-building events are a good thing. As a seasoned banker working with colleagues 20 years younger than me, I dread these events. I don't want to spend my precious weekends with co-workers the age of my kids, over-enthusiastic mediators and false bonhomie with people who I will still dislike on Monday morning.'

Ms Kellaway assured him that it was perfectly reasonable to decline the invitation. I would agree, but with an important caveat: it is absolutely essential to encourage close cooperation and teamwork within management and working teams more generally. The problem with away-days or activity weekends is that they can be too removed from the actual tasks and discussions you need to have as a working management team. It is more empowering to focus on the skills and conversations that will actually help you deliver. At LEGO, we had a highly effective coach and facilitator whose intervention helped the business turnaround. It certainly wasn't soft, it was actually quite tough at times. It was also highly effective in many respects, although it demonstrates the infinite complexity of the interactions of multiple teams and relationships in any business.

Summary

Nothing in a complex business is neatly divided. As former head of marketing Mads Nipper and I discovered at LEGO, operations, marketing and design have to be considered together. Not only is it impossible to separate a business into 'hard' and 'soft' disciplines, the more important learning is that they don't really exist. For some, the terms may be a useful shorthand for identifying different managerial disciplines; the danger lies in segregating these arbitrarily defined categories of the managerial task, which can result in team-building exercises that lack purpose and focus, and neglect of communication and relationship-building in technical or operational work.

Key principles from this chapter

- The concepts of 'hard' and 'soft' managerial disciplines are metaphors; they are arbitrary and can be unhelpful, especially when they lead to a segregation of relational and operational considerations.
- The way in which 'hard' managerial concepts have been used often leads to bureaucracy and complexity.
- It is better to unite the relational and operational, to keep an eye on the real business.
- The most motivational and engaging experience when working as a team is to collectively deliver what you promise, delighting the customer.

- Teams are only effective if the participants are genuinely committed to helping the business; at times, individual motivations can create distortions.

How to implement the principles

- Team-building exercises that are unconnected to the team's actual purpose and required skills can be ineffective. It is better to have interventions that directly support the teams.
- If the primary purpose of an event is for social bonding, better to have an unambiguously fun event.
- Intense, open conversations are often needed to build a multi-disciplinary team – especially during critical projects or in a turnaround situation. Different disciplines come with different mindsets. Professional facilitation can help.
- Try to understand someone's drive: if an individual is pushing for a certain project or initiative, try to find out why.

Chapter 13
Hidden Risks of Success

Many in the business world know that the LEGO company nearly went bust in the period 2002–04. Some famous brands have disappeared in the past 20 years and this one nearly did too. Its survival and recovery were not inevitable. While the company's strategic renewal is well known in business circles, the repair of the supply chain, equally essential for the turnaround, has not been, though this book tells a good part of the story. As you will by now appreciate, the rescue and subsequent revival of LEGO owed much to the recognition of CEO Jørgen Vig Knudstorp that the contribution of those of us in operations was central and that we were as capable of creating value as any other department.

In the early part of my 15-year career at LEGO, we had some tough calls to make. I acquired some nicknames that were mildly unflattering though rather jocular (at least, I hope so!). I was 'Mr Grumpy' or 'Dr No'. I disliked waste, lack of accountability and sloppiness; I insisted on zero errors in packing, reduction in supply chain complexity, relentless focus on the consumer's needs, all backed by the discipline of the Visual Factory. I do not believe that the company would have survived without these disciplines.

After we had turned the fortunes of the company around, and growth returned, I enjoyed being part of a dynamic success story. Yet the stresses of spectacular growth were higher than I expected. It presented problems that are known as 'good problems to have' – how to hire enough staff, how to ensure supply – but which are, nonetheless, challenges. I learned as much in these years as I did in the rescue phase. An organisation has hidden vulnerabilities at the zenith of its fortunes. Nothing is perfect, nothing lasts forever. Just as there is hope in every crisis, there is risk in every boom.

There is another common misleading belief that I have encountered in my career, which is that progress in business is linear and inevitable. In reality, it demands constant discipline. Not all change is good; management requires curation and nurturing, as well as innovation. Some human habits, including among highly intelligent and qualified people, can take a business off course, because none of us is free from ego, misjudgement, collective misunderstandings or the temptation of complacency. We may hire too many people. We begin initiatives that offer a personal legacy, or short-term but unsustainable financial gain, rather than help the business. We decline to question narratives that have become outdated because we're emotionally attached to approaches that are associated with past success.

By the mid-2010s, LEGO had been growing and profitable for a decade, led by an established leadership team headed by Jørgen Vig Knudstorp as CEO. Nothing, however, lasts forever. Mads Nipper, a brilliant and ambitious individual in sales and marketing, becoming chief marketing officer, was appointed in 2014 to a chief executive role at Grundfos, a Danish industrial firm that manufactures pumps and pumping equipment. By 2016, Jørgen had been CEO for more than ten years. Changes and growth within LEGO opened up new opportunities. The Kristiansen family wanted to create a new entity, called the LEGO Brand Group, to explore new innovations and investment opportunities, separate from the core company, similar to the relationship between the Alphabet group and Google.

LEGO is a single-brand firm. It is well-established business logic that innovating entirely new products within an established company is problematic: either energy and resources get sucked into the established brand, thwarting the new ventures, or the new initiatives become successful and the older products become neglected. It's generally better to spin off a new venture, or set up a different entity, for a new idea with a new name. The LEGO Brand Group would have the freedom to acquire companies, to invest in new opportunities opened up by technology, such as 3D printing, without the new enterprises becoming a distraction from, or in competition for resources with, the firm making the iconic range of LEGO toys. The lesson from the late 1990s, when diversification within the firm led to brand stretch and loss of direction, had been well learned. Jørgen had been identified as the proposed chair of this new entity, creating an opening for someone to be chief executive of the established LEGO Group. As he explained this to me over several conversations, it became increasingly clear that the individual the family had in mind was me – at least for an interim period. Generally, they preferred the internal promotion of an individual who knows 'the LEGO way'.

This was immensely satisfying and flattering. As with my first promotion at LEGO some 15 years earlier, I did not want a job title that included a term such as 'interim' or 'acting', which would convey a temporary air, with limited authority as staff await a permanent appointment, and this was agreed. Unofficially, I acknowledged that the appointment was for an extended interim period while the board sought a successor, but I argued that it would weaken the authority of the post to have a temporary-sounding title. There was a concern over my age, in that I had just turned 60. I did not regard this attitude of the board as ageist, because I had openly discussed the possibility of retiring soon after this landmark birthday. Through the years of long working hours and international travel I had missed my family so much that I had no intention of working full-time into my late 60s. I anticipated that the CEO role might last two to four years, enough for me to make something of an impact before moving to a comfortable retirement.

With Jørgen moving to a newly created post, and other senior level changes, choreographing the board level and executive roles took several months of negotiation but finally, in December 2016, the board announced that the first non-Danish chief executive of LEGO would be myself – a British-Asian alumnus of the Gordon School in Gravesend, who had left school at 17. The British and Indian news media loved this, of course, and my promotion attracted a fair amount of press coverage in the business pages.

LEGO is fun – for supply chain people also

I was, perhaps, the typical 'safe pair of hands' – a long-established insider with a background in operations. 'My' team in the supply chain were naturally delighted that one of their own had been appointed to the top role. In marketing and design there was, I sensed, some apprehension. To many in the business, I was still Mr Grumpy or Dr No. I never set out to be the bearer of bad news, it was just my policy that when I encountered it I would speak out about the problems and want them addressed. I loved the products as much as anyone in the business. Once in role, of course, I had to put aside any sense of loyalty to one department or another. As chief executive, I was responsible for all areas of the business.

Early in my LEGO career there had been numerous headaches: the supply problems, the data issues, the lack of transparency, the troubled outsourcing relationship. There was tension within my team and between my team and others. These issues, some of them presenting emergencies, dominated my early years with the company. Grappling with all this was essential for the company's very survival, especially in the early months of the turnaround. At times in those periods it was easy to forget that the product is about fun!

I love LEGO. While I may have challenged designers at times, I also admired their visual and engineering genius. I particularly admire their resilience: only a minority of ideas put forward by design teams can be accepted and converted into a product; yet they never complain, just return to producing something new for the following year. They do more than create new play experiences, they create new worlds for children of all ages to explore, expanding the minds and creative options for enquiring individuals the world over.

If you're unfamiliar with some of the more astounding products, it's worth spending a while online. You can encounter satirical stop animation videos with LEGO mini figures – for example, re-enactments of famous football matches, replete with the original commentary as soundtrack. The British comedian Eddie Izzard once did a brilliant sketch imagining the *Star Wars* villain Darth Vader on his lunch break in the staff canteen of the Death Star, trying to order *Penne al'arrabiata*, and becoming irritated because all the trays are wet. The video of an animated version with LEGO mini figures, accompanied by the original Eddie Izzard recording, is as funny as anything you can find on YouTube. I particularly enjoyed seeing Darth Vader brandish a conventional thin blue 3 x 2 LEGO brick as a canteen tray. The brick is instantly recognisable, ubiquitous – and the fact that it isn't shaped exactly like a canteen tray becomes part of the joke; if you were to substitute it with a realistic-looking item, the humour would fade a little. The animator displays a sophisticated understanding of how comedy works and how the audience views a common LEGO brick; and without doubt the viewers (more than 27m at the time of writing) are in on the joke. In this, and numerous other examples, the users of LEGO combine with the brilliant designers to create new videos, new worlds, new ideas. It becomes less a toy, more an opening into a new, imaginative universe.

Many celebrated architects, engineers and designers had their enthusiasm fired by building with LEGO as children, continuing as adults. This does not mean, of course, that

LEGO is only an educational tool, a means to an end: it is inherently playful and fun.

One point my team on the supply side had made throughout those years of crisis, recovery and renewed growth was the following: the company as a whole had no chance of enriching these users' lives unless we could convert the designers' creations into high-quality products and do so reliably and cost-effectively. An illustration of the necessity of engaging the entire enterprise comes from reflecting on the fact that, throughout the loss-making periods of failed products and disillusioned fans, through to the years of unbounded growth, LEGO movies and the like, we had predominantly the same designers in the same teams. The difference was the leadership and it was a leadership that saw the whole company as an ecosystem, with each element of equal importance.

This perspective was shared by the former head of marketing Mads Nipper, who in an interview for this book describes it as 'one of the most eye-opening leadership experiences that I have had in 30 years'. Mads was asked to return from a post in Germany to head the marketing function. He recalls: 'My incoming assumption was, with the crap products we have been doing now for three years and running, this is something that needs a fundamental turnaround, we need to replace 100s of people and stuff. But when I had dialogues with the leaders, but especially with the designers, they all knew what to do!'

Mads discovered that the problem was the direction from the top, not the skill level within the teams. He adds: 'I still remember [one designer], from the Technik team, he built the motorcycle, overnight. I think he worked all night. The fire truck . . . they built it. The prototype was built in days. We don't need a new strategy – I mean, just do what you see fit, and I still remember they came up with the Vikings play theme in literally a matter of weeks and had built prototypes. So, the organisation had all it took and I think we hardly let go of any people.'

As business results and job security improved, we could enjoy ourselves a little more, with occasional go-karting trips and the like. It was a relief to have moved out of the period of crisis. On another occasion, we arranged to have a short stop-animation video with mini figures representing ourselves in a satirical management conference – there was a multi-disciplinary effort to produce the short movie and it was hilarious.

Every year we would hold an internal conference for the top 100 or so people in the company to review and make plans for the year. It typically featured some kind of fun gift for delegates. In 2015 I commissioned a book called *Dear LEGO People*, which featured extracts from letters to the company written by children. They were endearing, often cheeky, at times funny, and above all, infused with creativity and with love for the product. One boy wrote in to request a free set in return for having spotted a typo on the packaging. Another asked that their least favourite character in the Ninjago series be killed off. One letter was addressed to 'Dear Mr and Mrs LEGO'. A creative young user sent in photographs, from different angles, of their own version of the Minions character – the little figures with yellow heads and goggle eyes from the movie franchise. The photo showed a LEGO Minion that was extra-wide and with unique features, neatly symmetrical, the child kindly offering to send us instructions on how to construct it. Many were signed off with the simple phrase: 'I love LEGO' – and there were several in which the letter-writer expressed a desire to become a LEGO designer when they were grown up. It was fascinating to see how engaged many of the children were with the storyline-themed toys – for example, Ninjago, with some missives offering sharply opinionated advice over which characters to develop more – or not! The book was only for internal use. As well as being enormous fun, the book gave fascinating insights into how our youngest fans loved building, playing and experimenting with the bricks.

Simplify to grow

The role of chief executive involved more than running the business; there was an ambassadorial dimension. While

LEGO is not Denmark's largest company – it is smaller than, for example, the Maersk shipping firm or pharmaceuticals firm Novo Nordisk – it is the most recognised, and the most revered – repeatedly voted the most-loved brand, or in the top five, year after year. As such, it is part of the country's identity and the responsibility for continuing that tradition is huge. The chief executive will be invited to be part of a trade delegation, accompanying ministers from the Danish government, for example; and there will be invitations to give speeches. My diary became full, rapidly. Internally, everyone wanted an audience and some individuals could express annoyance if I granted half an hour instead of two hours. I had two personal assistants, who were quite brilliant, as you would expect.

Another headache for a chief executive of LEGO is the perennial threat of counterfeiting and other potential breaches of intellectual property. In the early days of LEGO, the brick was covered by a patent and copying it was technically challenging. By the time I was chief executive, the patent had expired a long time earlier, in 1989. There was, however, one major success: with a legal case in China. Some of the efforts at counterfeit LEGO products, or competitors who we felt were copying rather than producing their own intellectual property, were of lesser quality, but a serious threat emerged when imitators in China began producing bricks of higher quality.

In the legal battle that followed, we were successful in the Chinese courts, forcing two companies producing imitation toy bricks to cease production. The ruling came in December 2017.[16]

For all that there were pressures as chief executive, especially as regards time, I regarded it as an opportunity, not a burden. There is more stress in being unemployed and poor than in holding a senior post. And there was a clear need, and opportunity for me, to build on our achievements in the years of success and create a platform for growth and innovation in the future. With my appointment as one for the short- to medium-term, the emphasis had to be on ensuring discipline and transparency – getting the basics right.

Although the company had been successful and growing for a decade, there were amber warning signs of potential trouble ahead. Growth in 2016 was weaker than previous years, costs were rising quicker than sales and profits, with headcount in particular rising sharply. Decision-making was slowing down and managerial structures were becoming more complex. For example, we had set up a mechanism for approving investments, but it had become so laborious that decisions were not being made. Yet while people were waiting for decisions, hiring continued and with it, managerial complexity. My view was that there should be no more than six levels between the CEO and the blue-collar individual working on an operating line, but when I analysed the situation, it had grown to eight or even nine levels.

Such features almost inevitably creep in when a business is thriving over an extended period of time. Yves Morieux, a consultant from the Boston Consulting Group who advised us, used the metaphor of the 'Second TV', a problem that accompanies prosperity. It refers to how a family in previous eras before video recorders and with only one TV would have to discuss and debate with each other which channel to watch. As devices become more common and families become wealthier, everyone acquires their own TV in their bedroom, which is convenient, but it means that there is less discussion. In the context of a company, the 'Second TV' – a saying we would use in LEGO after Yves' input – was a warning about not holding sufficient debate and scrutiny over spending increases and consequent lapses in self-discipline.

Hollywood arrives and the brand goes stratospheric

Success tends to breed success. Such was the high profile of the LEGO brand that, in the 2010s, Hollywood came knocking. The legendary studio Warner Brothers wanted to make a LEGO movie, the Kristiansen family agreed and the studio hired the best talent in writing, acting and special effects. The release – *The LEGO Movie* – was in 2014 and was well received by critics and families alike. It was filled with action, a LEGO Batman mini figure, was genuinely funny and featured an A-list cast providing the voices, among them Morgan Freeman, Elizabeth Banks, Will Ferrell and Liam Neeson. The movie was a hit and spawned a sequel. Earlier franchise agreements with *Star Wars* and *Harry Potter* were still in place. There was a further LEGO movie based on the Ninjago TV series and martial arts-themed LEGO toys that we had launched in 2011. The critical reception was slightly less enthusiastic, but it still kept the LEGO brand high in the public gaze. Sales of LEGO toys, already strong, rocketed. For us on the supply side, it turned out to be absolutely crazy.

To give an illustration of the type of growth we were engaged in: to begin with in the Mexico manufacturing plant, we had 50 machines running. Quickly, this became 120, and within 18 months, we had 768. Even with this growth in capacity, we weren't always keeping up with demand. Scaling was the biggest challenge we had. There was constant hiring and ensuring you recruit the right people becomes a high priority. We had learned some useful tips from Flextronics, our manufacturing outsourcing partner in the period 2005–08, on how to adopt hiring tactics at scale, including of temporary staff, to help scaling up. For all that the world was becoming more online and digital, there was still a desire for play that involved creativity and the sense of touch.

The phrase 'constant paranoia' is sometimes extolled in management circles, including in my time at LEGO, to guard against complacency. It can be helpful, yet we discovered that finding the sweet spot between caution and over-confidence can be tricky. We ended up being too conservative in our investing in some years, although this was only obvious in hindsight. At times in the 2010s demand for LEGO toys was growing at around 15–25 per cent, year on year. We would tell ourselves: 'It's not going to happen again next year.' But then it did. Success is temporary, but it can be difficult to detect whether a trend will last six months or six years.

David Haigh, CEO of Brand Finance, described why LEGO was ranked the most powerful brand in 2017, writing in the UK journal *Finance Monthly*: 'The firm [LEGO] has clearly been at pains to rebuild and preserve the strength of its brand. This can be achieved with an ultra-conservative approach . . . however that leads to missed opportunities for credible brand extension that could generate huge returns. In contrast, LEGO has invested heavily in research, providing a thorough understanding of what underpins brand strength, so that commercial opportunities can be pursued without compromising the brand.'[17]

Yet success is never permanent, nor complete. Humans are restless beings. Whoever said that 'people hate change' was seriously wrong; we are easily bored and constantly crave new stimuli. One of the problems of success is complacency and the arrogance that can follow, while another is that success can become a bit boring, prompting restless executives to seek new initiatives. In steady-state, successful periods, if a new executive comes in, they often want a big initiative associated with them: a project that brings with it a sense of emotional ownership. So, there is a temptation that, rather than doing the right thing for the company, people start to do things to make a name for themselves.

The board could see that I had the skills well-suited for the kind of correction necessary. The ability to say 'no', an emphasis on transparency, simplicity of managerial structure and avoidance of waste were my strengths. Appointing me was akin to the company going on a diet and taking up exercise. With the board, we decided upon an initiative called 'Simplify to Grow'. One of the earliest decisions I made was to disband the large leadership team of 22 individuals, which had been a logical idea but which, in practice, was too unwieldy for many decisions that we had to make. Another was to trim some of the excesses that had sprung up during the years of growth.

A discipline I liked to encourage during growth periods was: 'Do not install tomorrow's cost-cutting opportunities today'. At times this meant pushing back with certain departments and with the HR function, who had supported the tendency to engage quite freely in hiring new staff. I tried to encourage HR to question a function when it said that it needed to create a new post – to be rigorous in pressing for a business case. This type of approach, I discovered, does not come naturally to HR professionals, though I feel I made some progress in this area. I had already taken over responsibility for HR, since 2014, as chief operations officer, and introduced something similar to the Visual Factory there. The presenting problem had been that, as high growth continued, we had been struggling to recruit staff in sufficient numbers and quality, so we introduced some of the same disciplines for HR that we had introduced for the supply chain some years earlier. This meant more focus and clarity around what we needed to do, in terms of identifying talent, filling posts, matching supply and demand. There had been a problem in scaling up, hiring enough talent to fill positions, but within a few months of introducing the Visual Factory, we had caught up. What was needed subsequently was greater rigour to ensure the justifiability of each hire.

With the 'Simplify to Grow' initiative, there was a neat continuity with the achievements we had realised in operations. We had helped transform the culture to improve performance, transparency and accountability by the simple but radical innovation of the White Board meetings, the Visual Factory. I could see that my most valuable contribution while chief executive was to strengthen and prolong this.

Maintaining the culture

While there was a necessary focus on tasks and accountability, it is always necessary to balance the 'what' of execution with the 'how'; that is, to ensure that people are always treated with dignity and respect. A task-focused culture in which targets are reached, customer demands met, financial performance is strong, will be unsustainable if people feel burnt out or taken for granted. So, in monitoring performance, including annual reviews, we sought to maintain this balanced approach.

Throughout my career at LEGO, I had learned to be a better listener. Even when I felt I had a strong case, backed by evidence, I discovered that it is often worth the effort to listen closely to an alternative point of view. It was a difficult adjustment for me because when I had begun my career in 2002, LEGO was in a state of crisis. Many of my colleagues were in denial about the scale of the crisis. The very survival of the company was at stake and there wasn't much time for listening. As growth returned, I adjusted my style to become more listening, coaching and collaborative. More than one person suggested as a consequence that I was not consistent! To which I was tempted to reply, as Brian said to the beggar he gave money to in the Monty Python movie *Life of Brian*: 'There's no pleasing some people!'

Hidden Risks of Success

Our ambition on the operations side at LEGO, throughout the whole period from the 2003–04 crisis years for the following decade, was to make operations a source of competitive advantage, rooted in reconstructing the firm around the concept of LEGO as a system of play, increasing the proportion of common components, radically improving effectiveness of the supply chain and effectively matching supply with demand. This approach supported and nurtured innovation and the continual increase of demand for our fun products. The modular building system, universally recognised and popular, could be used as a basis for unleashing successive waves of exciting new toys, each using a high proportion of common components – simultaneously delighting the consumers, keeping costs low and margins high. Within this system of play, exciting new functions using digital components could be incorporated. It was a case of a 'both/and' approach to digital and the brick, not an 'either/or'.

And we succeeded. We succeeded completely and for a sustained period of time – beyond our expectations. The central, strategic contribution of operations both to the turnaround and the decade of growth that followed was something that Jørgen Vig Knudstorp understood while he was CEO. I saw my promotion as recognition of this and I sought to use my new role to build on our successes.

Summary

A leading executive role throws up some surprising challenges during years of strong profit margins and growth. It becomes harder and harder to say 'no' to a project you feel is ill-advised or unnecessary, because you cannot fall back on the argument that 'we cannot afford it'. It often feels uncomfortable to say 'no' to someone, especially if it means deflating their enthusiasm for a while. Doing so, however, creates opportunities too, releasing resources for projects that the leadership team judge to be more worthwhile. Such a judgement will never be a precise science, but business leaders have to make these calls, some more impactful than others. The survival, turnaround and success at LEGO indicates that those of us overseeing the transition must have made far more correct decisions than poor ones and worked hard to ensure implementation.

Key principles from this chapter

- Understanding the talent deployed is important: the design and operational teams employed during a period of losses and difficulty at a firm may be able to contribute to success with better leadership.
- Being a senior executive during a period of growth can be surprisingly challenging as complexity tends to grow and there can be temptations to indulge in risky or unnecessary investments.

- Scaling up is a huge challenge if demand takes off.
- Saying 'no' to a project is difficult but often necessary in order to keep focused on the potential for real growth in demand.
- A different managerial style is dominant during a turnaround compared with revival and growth.

How to implement the principles

- Do not implement tomorrow's cost-cutting opportunities today. Remember that wasteful practices will always harm a business.
- A leader should look ahead: if a business is profitable, but margins are being reduced and waste is creeping in, better to head off the problems than wait for crisis to hit.
- As you move out of crisis and into growth, it's important to listen more and move from a directing to a more coaching style of leadership.
- When scaling up, it's essential to have a very business-focused HR function, to ensure the right people are being hired, often rapidly to maintain growth.

Afterword

As it turned out, my tenure as CEO was rather more interim than I had expected. When Jørgen Vig Knudstorp invited me for a meeting in late 2017 and opened it by saying: 'This is going to be a difficult conversation . . .' I knew what was coming. The official explanation was that they had identified their ideal successor rather sooner than anticipated and that may have been the whole of the story.

I would have found it more rewarding to have been in place long enough to see the outcome of the 'Simplify to Grow' initiative, and to leave at a time more of my choosing, but overall, I could look back with immense satisfaction at a 15-year career at the firm, during which it could not be disputed that I had played a central role in its survival, turnaround and recovery. I could leave with my head held high and true to the example I had witnessed with the Enfield staff a decade earlier, I was diligent in handing over to my successor.

My departure was handled in a rather abrupt manner. There was no celebratory farewell dinner, with my family invited, that I could reasonably have expected, of the kind that I had arranged for senior retiring executives. Jørgen gave a glowing tribute at my farewell do, but it was a modest, mid-morning affair. It all felt a little flat after the significant contribution I had made over the years to the company's survival and subsequent prosperity. My personal effects were transported to our home in Gravesend. I felt a certain awkwardness at the lack of ceremony and the timing, in that if a CEO is replaced in such a manner a little less than a year into the tenure, it would usually be because of some impropriety or poor performance, so the most painful aspect for me of the departure was the speculation it provoked. Even my wife Sati, when I returned home, said: 'You must have done something. What have you done?'

'Nothing, dear, nothing!' I protested.

Probably, there had been some politics at board level, some manoeuvring for my departure, of which I was unaware. I considered it futile then, as now, to speculate on its precise nature, to dig for the 'real' reason for my abrupt and, I would argue, premature replacement, and preferred to reflect on an overall successful tenure. So, feeling proud and somewhat piqued, I settled with Sati into our shared retirement. For a while, the job offers poured in – not least from Chinese toy manufacturers and private equity firms invested in the toy sector – but I had no desire to return to a full-time post, instead becoming a part-time consultant and enjoying a semi-retirement. I could take out the golf clubs far more often, enjoy Sati's delicious Punjabi cuisine, be available for our children, whom I had missed so much during the hyper-busy executive years, and who were by this time grown-up and thriving; go for a spin through the Kent countryside in the E-Type Jaguar from time to time, glad to put an end to hotel living and jet lag.

Since stepping down as CEO of LEGO in 2017, I have continued to follow developments in management and take on consulting clients – often I've been appointed by investors to coach inexperienced CEOs heading start-ups. Many of them will know more than me about emerging technologies, but one of the fascinating aspects is that many of the recurring problems that they have to resolve are the perennial problems of management that this book covers: getting the teams right, the sense of purpose, the communication, the relevant data, the ability to coordinate and deliver; leaders who can do management and managers who can lead.

These disciplines will never go out of fashion. In a similar way, at LEGO in the early twenty-first century, we discovered that the humble brick was not becoming obsolete in the digital age – as had appeared to be the case – but instead was on the verge of a quite astonishing rebound in popularity. The impulse – the need, for many – to use one's hands in tactile play as a spur to creativity, imagination and pure joy is timeless. The discovery by our research and marketing teams that the types of LEGO sets that appeal to people around the world do not vary according to region or culture makes the brick-building activity a rather beautiful bonding experience for all of humanity (sadly, so is the pain when a barefoot parent treads on a brick left on the carpet; perhaps there are some problems we cannot solve!).

To continue delivering LEGO kits to the high quality that their millions of users around the world expect means continuing to deliver on the relentless discipline that management involves and which is common to all organisations. I hope this book helps your own business to deliver and your career to thrive.

Acknowledgements

Philip Whiteley for the help with writing, editing, phrasing and challenging me to tell the story so that it flows.

I have had the good fortune to have a number of mentors and coaches through out my career. A special call out to Keith Oliver (Booz Allen), Yves Morieux (BCG), Ian McCubbin (GSK), David Smith (Wellcome Foundation) and Jørgen Vig Knudstorp (LEGO).

I would like to extend deep gratitude to those who took time out of their busy schedules to help me formulate the book – Mads Nipper, Niels Duedahl, Paul Ferarrio, Tony Fadell, Jules Goddard, Yves Morieux.

In addition, thanks are due to the many colleagues with whom I had the good fortune to work alongside during the early days, and who continued the journey with me for a number of years. Just to name a few – Heather Manchester, Roger Vogt, Skip Kodak, Carsten Rasmussen, Michael Kehlet, Claus Pejstrup, John Hansen, Ole Therkilsen and the whole mould engineering team – the best engineers in the world!; Janet Kroes, Morten Pedersen, Thomas Nielsen, Alec Gowan, Simon Riis Hansen, Lone Andersen, Jesper Mikklesen – the best finance partner with a marketing education, and Helene Hartvig Nielsen for the best professional support I could have asked for during the difficult days.

Notes

1 Huang et al., 'How Customer Service Can Turn Angry Customers into Loyal Ones', *Harvard Business Review*, January 2018 https://hbr.org/2018/01/how-customer-service-can-turn-angry-customers-into-loyal-ones

2 'What happens to investors when a P2P firm collapses?', Altfi online journal, 2nd March, 2018 https://www.altfi.com/article/4128_tales_of_failed_peer_to_peer_lenders

3 A brief summary of the Deming principles can be found at the following link: https://deming.org/explore/fourteen-points/ However, as this post explains, it is necessary to read a Deming textbook to have a full understanding of the approach. The 14 Deming principles, 'a system of profound knowledge' were first articulated in the title *Out of the Crisis* (MIT Press 1982, reissued 2018). *The New Economics* (MIT Press) was published in 1993.

4 'The High Cost of Poor Succession Planning: A better way to find your next CEO', Claudio Fernández-Aráoz,

Gregory Nagel and Carrie Green, *Harvard Business Review*, pp. 98–107, May–June 2021.

5 'Jeff Immelt shares out blame for GE's decline', *Financial Times*, Andrew Edgecliffe Johnson and Sujeet Indap, 26th February, 2021 https://www.ft.com/content/a64c4356-a42e-4883-acdb-13ced2bdcaea

6 'Why good strategies fail: Lessons for the C-Suite', Economist Intelligence Unit, July 2013 https://perspectives.eiu.com/strategy-leadership/why-good-strategies-fail

7 'Education: Historical statistics', House of Commons, 27th November, 2012, file:///C:/Users/DELL/Downloads/SN04252.pdf

8 Kenyon-Rouvinez, D., 'Secrets of success in long-lasting family firms', IMD, June 2017 https://www1.imd.org/research-knowledge/articles/secrets-of-success-in-long-lasting-family-firms/ *See also* Osnes, G. (ed) *Family Capitalism: Best practices in ownership and leadership*, Routledge 2016.

9 The LEGO Case Study 2014 by John Ashcroft and Company.

10 A summary of retail trends in the toy sector in USA in the 1990s and early 2000s, published in 2013, was produced by industry research organisation IBIS World: https://www.ibisworld.com/industry-insider/industry-insights/hobby-toy-stores-the-game-has-changed/

Notes

11 'Interest in Puzzles Soars, Along With Sales', *AARP*, 18th May, 2020, https://www.aarp.org/home-family/friends-family/info-2020/puzzles-sales-soar.html *See also* 'Vinyl Record Sales Top Compact Discs for First Time in 34 Years', Bloomberg, 10th September, 2020 https://www.bloomberg.com/news/articles/2020-09-10/vinyl-record-sales-top-compact-discs-for-first-time-in-34-years

12 'How Amazon Survived the Dot-Com Crash to Rule the Cloud', eWEEK, 27th December, 2013 https://www.eweek.com/cloud/eweek-at-30-how-amazon-survived-the-dot-com-crash-to-rule-the-cloud

13 Weeks, M., Freeny, David F., 'Outsourcing: From Cost Management to Innovation and Business Value', *California Management Review*, 1st July, 2008 https://journals.sagepub.com/doi/abs/10.2307/41166459?journalCode=cmra

14 Sanders, N. R. and Wood, J. D., 'The Secret to AI is People', *Harvard Business Review*, 24th August, 2020, https://hbr.org/2020/08/the-secret-to-ai-is-people

15 Yves Morieux, 'As work gets more complex: six rules to simplify', TED Talk, uploaded 23rd January, 2014 https://www.youtube.com/watch?v=0MD4Ymjyc2I&t=99s

16 'Lego wins its first Chinese legal case against imitators', *CBS News*, 7th December, 2017 https://www.cbsnews.com/news/lego-wins-its-first-chinese-legal-case-against-imitators/

17 'Why is LEGO the most powerful brand in the world?' *Finance Monthly*, 8th February, 2017 https://www.finance-monthly.com/2017/02/why-is-lego-the-most-powerful-brand-in-the-world/

Index

Index

Index

Business and smart-thinking books for curious readers and business leaders.

Designed to inspire, energise, and encourage.

Heligo
Books

Sign-up for exclusive content:
www.heligobooks.co.uk